"Clear, concise, and clever—both in the sense of giving you counter-intuitive ideas and being fun to read. If this won't get them to pay attention, I don't know what will."

—John A. Byrne, executive editor, *BusinessWeek*

"Okay, so it wasn't until I was at 35,000 feet with the BlackBerry out of range and the laptop battery dead that I was able to focus my attention on *Your Attention, Please*. And I'm glad I did. Paul B. Brown and Alison Davis provide a wealth of easy-to-follow ways to more effectively reach your audience. *Your Attention, Please.* is informative, useful, and yes, even funny. I've never made a book required reading for my team, until now."

—Steven T. Church, Senior Director, Communication, Georgia-Pacific

"How do you communicate with an audience that is overworked, over stimulated, and overloaded with information? By telling them a story they want to hear. Brown and Davis lay out the dos and don'ts of creating a compelling story that breaks through all the clutter. *Your Attention, Please.* is a good story that will help you and your audience be more effective."

—Bill Linton, Director of New Product Development, Bush Brothers

"It's true: Everyone is communicating, but no one is listening. In *Your Attention, Please.*, Alison Davis and Paul B. Brown reveal the clean little secrets of getting your message across—Keep it Simple, Keep it Short, and Keep it Smart. Successful politicians do it: 'It's Morning in America.' Hollywood can do it even shorter: 'Die Harder.' Madison Avenue can likewise Different.' But I can do it in one word

olumnist

YOUR ATTENTION, PLEASE.

How to Appeal to Today's
Distracted, Disinterested,
Disengaged, Disenchanted,
and Busy Consumer

Paul B. Brown and Alison Davis

AVON, MASSACHUSETTS

Published by Adams Media, an F+W Publications Company
57 Littlefield Street
Avon, MA 02322
www.adamsmedia.com

ISBN 10: 1-59337-687-1
ISBN 13: 978-1-59337-687-1

Printed in the United States of America.

J   I   H   G   F   E   D   C   B   A

Library of Congress Cataloging-in-Publication Data
Brown, Paul B.
Your attention, please. / by Paul B. Brown and Alison Davis.
p.   cm.
ISBN 1-59337-687-1
1. Advertising—Psychological aspects. 2. Attention. I. Davis, Alison (Alison Bonnie)
II. Title.
HF5822.B82 2006
659.1—dc22
2006014721

This publication is designed to provide accurate and authoritative information with regard to the subject matter covered. It is sold with the understanding that the publisher is not engaged in rendering legal, accounting, or other professional advice. If legal advice or other expert assistance is required, the services of a competent professional person should be sought.

> —From a *Declaration of Principles* jointly adopted by a Committee of the
> American Bar Association and a Committee of Publishers and Associations

Many of the designations used by manufacturers and sellers to distinguish their product are claimed as trademarks. Where those designations appear in this book and Adams Media was aware of a trademark claim, the designations have been printed with initial capital letters.

This book is available at quantity discounts for bulk purchases.
For information, please call 1-800-872-5627.

Contents

Putting These Ideas into Practice

INTRODUCTION

This book is for you if:

- Your success depends on your ability to communicate effectively.
- You are finding it increasingly difficult to get people's attention.
- You know—or suspect—that people are tuning out without getting your message, much less acting on it.

At this moment, all across America, there are millions of people just like you—people who need to communicate to achieve their objectives. Maybe you're a professional communicator. Or a manager. Or someone in marketing or sales who needs to get through to customers or prospects. Or a human resources professional. Or a senior leader who needs to excite and engage your work force.

Whatever your role, you're probably feeling increasingly frustrated.

Your audience is so busy, and so overloaded with communication coming at them from all directions—e-mails, memos, voice mail, company publications and reports, sales updates, the latest government reporting regulations, industry trade publications (the list seems endless because it is)—that they barely glance at whatever materials you send them.

Tuning out and turning off

You're know you're not capturing people's attention when they:

✓ Delete e-mails without reading them.

✓ Ignore, or at best skim, printed materials.

✓ Zone out during presentations.

✓ Fast-forward through voice mails and videos.

✓ Fail to retain the meaning of what you're communicating.

At best, they're reluctant—at worst, they're downright hostile when it comes to paying attention to what you have to say. They're cranky because they're besieged by communication that isn't relevant to them.

As a result, no matter how hard you work to get your message right, it just isn't working.

Maybe you need to stop struggling so much. Maybe what you need is a radically different approach.

That's where we come in. We understand your pain—we're communicators, too. We've struggled with that horrible sinking feeling of knowing that even though our message was sound and our writing was clear, it still wasn't working: We weren't grabbing the attention of the people we needed to reach.

That's when we decided to reinvent what we do. We stopped typing and started looking around at how the world had changed, and how our customers' expectations had changed along with it. We studied what experts in

◀◀ We understand your pain—we're communicators, too.

psychology, marketing, adult learning, and other fields had discovered about people's attention spans, comprehension, and motivation. We left our comfort zone and entered the sometimes scary world of gossip magazines, video games, blogs, and tried to decipher our teenagers' text messages.

We analyzed survey data that indicates how people are experiencing all forms of communication, from network television to personal e-mails. And we interviewed people: employees, customers, and other target audiences; people of all ages—in their 60s, 50s, 40s, 30s, 20s, even the afore-mentioned teenagers (talk about scary!).

What we learned

We discovered 3 critical facts about today's audience:

1. *People won't pay attention to information just because it's interesting.* There's so much good communication

Who are we?

Alison has spent the last 20 years running a company whose sole function is to help companies such as Aetna, Dow Corning, Hewlett-Packard, Johnson & Johnson, Raytheon, and Wyeth communicate with their employees. (And employees are the world's #2 toughest audience—the toughest, of course, is teenagers.)

Paul has been a writer for more years than he would care to admit, working for publications—such as *BusinessWeek, Fast Company,* and the *New York Times*—whose business it is to capture readers' attention. He's also written a book or 2 (actually, 15) along the way.

Together, we have figured out what works to reach today's busy distracted audiences.

available that "interesting" is simply the starting point for attracting people's interest. To get your audience to pick up your brochure or keep their itchy fingers from hitting the "delete" button, you've got to go much, much further: Exciting. Fun. Immediate. Compelling. Useful. And, most of all, relevant (see #2).

◀◀ Exciting. Fun. Immediate. Compelling. Useful. And, most of all, relevant.

2. *The most relevant communication is "all about me"— information that directly relates to audience members' needs and wants.* Your audience members might be so stressed out their heads feel like they're exploding, but they'll still stop and pay attention when someone says:

- "This is for you."
- "Here's something that can help you."
- "You can be (thinner, richer, happier). Here's how."

3. *No matter how compelling (#1) or personally relevant (#2) your communication might be, your audience won't pay attention if they have to work too hard.* The media (TV, radio, newspapers, magazines, Internet) has set the expectation that communication will be as easy as the Toll House cookie "mixes" Nestlé sells in the supermarket dairy aisle: You don't have to "mix" anything; just open the package, plop the dough on a pan, bake, and presto! "Homemade" cookies!

Unless your communication is just as easy to use— accessible, easy to navigate, quick to digest, and completely clear—your audience won't participate. To continue the cookie metaphor, people may glance at the recipe but they

How easy is this?

The mainstream media is dedicated to making it easy for the audience to get what it needs quickly and easily. For instance, consider these energy-saving techniques from the world of television:

- The TV remote control.
- During football or baseball games, the little boxes that show pertinent facts and statistics.
- Headlines "crawling" across the bottom of a CNN *Headline News* broadcast.

"What do we need to do differently to get a message across to today's busy and distracted audiences?" ▶▶

just won't take the time to measure flour, cream butter, and mix up the batter. By the time you notice that your audience isn't paying attention, they've already left the kitchen. (It's telling that most people don't buy cookbooks to actually prepare food, but as culinary coffee table books.)

The bottom line

Based on what we learned about today's audiences, we started fresh and asked, "What do we need to do differently to get a message across to today's busy and distracted audiences?"

The answer was: Almost everything.

So we started creating a new formula for communication, one that is not based on old assumptions about people's attention, but one that deals with the reality of today. This book shares what we've learned in depth. The big-picture concepts include:

- Communication must quickly and obviously meet the needs of your audience. What you're sharing or selling cannot be about you—the person communicating, the company, or the product; it has to be about them.

- Your audience expects to find what they need immediately. They don't want to wander up and down the aisles of your communication store, searching for the refried beans they need to make dinner; they want a map, a sign—or even better, for someone to take them by the hand and lead them right to the information they seek.
- You don't have the luxury of time or patience. Remember Veruca Salt, the character in the movie *Willie Wonka and the Chocolate Factory*? She was the spoiled brat who said, "I want it and I want it now!" Everyone in your audience is like that, not because they've had indulgent parents—your audience simply doesn't have a choice. They're so beleaguered and overstimulated that they need it now.
- We assume you're a good communicator and can put together a decent sentence. But to quote TV chef Emeril Lagasse, "Now we need to kick it up a notch." Your communication needs to be punchier. More compelling. More vivid. And, most importantly, much shorter. In this competitive communication environment, we need to elevate our communication skills to new heights. We need to write better. Use visuals effectively. Organize everything logically and intuitively.

How this book will help you

We're going to show you how to create compelling communication. The kind of communication that grabs your audience member by the shirt collar, briskly slaps him across the cheekbone, and leaves him saying, "Thanks, I needed that!" This book is designed to:

- Practice what we preach. We'll demonstrate the techniques we advocate.
- Show examples of what to do and especially what *not* to do.
- Help you right now. There won't be a lot of theory you have to contemplate. This is advice you can put into action immediately.

Keep in mind:

This book is for you.

Whether you read every word or skim to find the best nuggets, the book is set up to give you the confidence and the tools you need to be successful at getting through to people.

We know you can do it, so let's get started.

Section 1
What's the Problem?

1 | Stuffed with information and starved for attention

Why don't people pay attention to your communication? Because, as this chapter explains, they're overloaded with information—so overwhelmed that they've lost their ability to focus.

IT MAY SEEM INCREDIBLE, but the information age is only about 25 years old. Today we can barely remember a time before personal computers, PDAs (personal digital assistants), digital cable, TiVo, iPods, camera cellphones, and all the other devices that bring us a constant and unending flood of data. But, in fact, all of these are younger than the 29-year-old in the next cubicle, who's spending his lunch hour playing online poker.

In the golden age before all this stuff made us both very entertained and very overwhelmed, people actually welcomed and treasured communication.

◀◀ People used to welcome and treasure communication.

Back then:

- In the morning, folks lingered over the daily newspaper. In the evening, they watched their favorite network television shows, getting up only to change the channel.
- At work, people paid careful attention to the memos, reports, and publications delivered to their inboxes.
- As customers, they were interested in ads, direct mailers, and other information that could entertain them or help them make a decision.

And then on
June 1, 1980, it all
began to unravel. ▶▶

In general, people were patient, tolerant, and even passive when it came to communication. They were busy, for sure, but they had the time to listen, to read, and to absorb.

And then on June 1, 1980, it all began to unravel.

That was the day CNN went on the air, and its access and immediacy ("Do you mean I can turn on the TV at 3:00 in the morning and find out what's going on anywhere in the world?") was the beginning of a communication revolution.

More, more, more

All these communication channels have created a mind-boggling volume of information—so much so, in fact, that analysts have to use measures of data like "terabytes" (1,000,000,000,000 bytes).

For example, according to the School of Information Management and Systems at the University of California at Berkeley:

- The Internet contains about 170 terabytes of information, which is 17 times more information than the Library of Congress print collections.
- In 2002, more than 31 billion e-mails were sent every day; by 2006, that volume is expected to double. E-mail generates about 400,000 terabytes of new information every year. (A typical academic research library contains about 2 terabytes of information.)
- There are about 5 billion instant messages per day, or 274 terabytes a year. (In the United States, 53 million people—4 in 10—use instant messaging, according to the Pew Internet & American Life Project, a nonprofit research organization.)

HOW THE WORLD CHANGED FOREVER

Year	Event	Why it changed the way we experience communication
1980	CNN is launched, introducing 24-hour-a-day news coverage.	Provides first access to events as they occur: Watch it live, don't read or hear about it later Creates universal experience (CNN is now available in 86% of American households).
1981	MTV debuts (with Video Killed The Radio Star).	Changes music, demonstrates that TV can be fun: ▶ Fast-moving ▶ Cool, hip ▶ Visual
1982	*USA Today* introduced.	Sets new standard for newspapers: ▶ Colorful ▶ Easy, predictable navigation ▶ Short, snappy copy ▶ Reader-oriented; "consumer-y"
1984	Internet domain name system established. Today 74% of Americans use the Internet an average of 11.1 hours per week. Most popular activities: ▶ Web surfing (76%) ▶ Reading news (51%) ▶ Entertainment (46%) ▶ Shopping (44%)	Communication expectations are changed forever: ▶ All doors are open—to information, products, services ▶ Users control the experience. You can get a little information, a lot, or anything in between ▶ "Reading" on screen = skimming
1989	Electronic Arts launches the "Madden NFL Football" video game, the first realistic sports game. By 2003, more than 30 million copies were sold.	Consumers are not watching the game; they're playing the game: ▶ Americans spent more time in 2003 playing video games—about 75 hours on average—than on watching rented videos and DVDs ▶ Average gamer is 29 years old; 44% female
1996	Instant messaging introduced. Today: ▶ 90% of 13- to 21-year olds instant message ▶ 43% of workers use instant messaging on the job	Communication as conversation: ▶ Writing or talking? (Are they the same thing?)

- The largest electronic channel for communication is the telephone: landlines and mobile phones. 98 percent of all information transmitted electronically occurs by phone.

Dead trees

Lest you think the information explosion is all digital, read facts from the old-fashioned world of print communication:

- A typical issue of the *New York Times* contains more information than the average person in the seventeenth century was likely to encounter during his entire lifetime.
- There were 18,821 magazines published in 2004, with a total of 156,586 pages of editorial content (including 23,766 pages devoted to celebrities, 10,364 to business, and 2,216 to consumer electronics).

You've got mail

Americans have a love/hate relationship with e-mail. On the one hand, we're addicted to it, saying that we rely on e-mail as much as we do on the telephone for communication and spending about an hour a day reading and writing e-mail, according to a study conducted by Opinion Research Corporation. Forty-one percent of Americans check their e-mail first thing in the morning, and 40 percent have checked their e-mail in the middle of the night.

But people find the volume of e-mail overwhelming, especially when it comes to unsolicited e-mail like spam. According to Pew, 70 percent of e-mail users say spam has made being online unpleasant or annoying, and 75 percent say they are bothered that they can't stop the flow of spam.

Still, no matter how annoying your problem is, you can take comfort in the fact that it's not as bad as the overload suffered by Bill Gates, the chairman of Microsoft Corporation. Mr. Gates receives 4 million e-mails per day, most of them spam.

" **What information consumes is rather obvious: it consumes the attention of its recipients. Hence a wealth of information creates a poverty of attention. "**

Herbert Simon,
the late Nobel laureate economist

- The United States Postal Service delivered 206 billion pieces of mail in 2004, including 97 billion first-class letters and packages and 9 billion periodicals.
- The largest production of print information occurs through the creation of office documents, which occurs mainly at office printers, according to U.C. Berkeley. Each person in North America consumes 11,916 sheets or 24 reams of paper each year.

Stop the madness

As a result of this data, your audience is beyond lightly toasted by information overload: They're completely cooked. Their only response is to desperately try to stop the madness by just saying no. People are reading, reading, reading, but retaining very little. Information is so plentiful and so disposable that it's become ephemeral. The meaning drifts off on the slightest breeze. People try to pin it down by printing out the information, putting it in a stack of paper to read later, throwing it in their briefcase to deal with at home. But, life at home isn't any more tranquil and because their brains are so overstimulated, they never fully focus.

Attention dysfunction

Being overwhelmed by information is not just an annoyance; it's an affliction. In fact, in modern America almost everyone suffers from at least one of these 5 attention ailments, which are described in ascending order of severity.

1. Multitasking mania

It's hard to find anyone these days who doesn't multitask: Reading the newspaper while watching TV. Dealing

---

⚠ JUST SAYING NO

People will delete e-mails without reading them—and not just the ones promising to improve their sex life or provide sure-fire investments—but those from the CEO ("It's probably not directly relevant."), retail companies they respect and do business with ("Looks like a great sale but I don't have time this week."), and professional associations ("Not now.") Or they do a "delayed delete": They leave the e-mails in their inbox to "read later" or file them in a folder, never to be referred to again.

---

with e-mails while on a conference call. Or our favorite: Sending messages on a BlackBerry while driving. (And people are worried about cell phones!)

PERCENT OF PEOPLE WHO MULTITASK WHILE:
Going online 69.3%
Listening to radio 69%
Watching TV 68.1%
Opening the mail 49.5%
Reading a newspaper 40.9%
Reading a magazine 40.2%

◀◀ Source: BIGresearch, 2005

Multitasking may seem like a sane approach to dealing with overload, but it's a form of mania. It creates a sense that everything is being speedily and simultaneously accomplished, while the reality is that nothing is being done

FedEx to nowhere . . .

Our favorite example of this new approach to dealing with mail was when we were sitting in a client's office and noticed a small stack of FedEx Overnight envelopes addressed to him sitting on the floor. Being curious (and forward), we asked, "What are those?" Turns out they were follow-up mailings from agencies the client had met at a professional association. The client was interested in their services—he invited the agencies to send him more material—but when the packages arrived, he never opened them. "I keep meaning to get to them," he said, somewhat sheepishly. Did it matter that the packages were mailed FedEx, which denotes some immediacy? "No. Everyone uses FedEx now, so that doesn't have any impact on when I open the packages."

well or completely. Multitasking leaves people with the empty feeling of having nothing to show for their time.

2. Hyperchoice syndrome

Is more always more? Not when it comes to your overloaded audience. Rather than making people feel empowered, too many options lead to entropy: With too many decisions to make, fatigue sets in, and people end up taking the easy (or familiar) way out. Think about how you watch cable or satellite TV—with hundreds of channels to choose from, how many have you actually watched?

We love this description of hyperchoice from David Mick, professor of marketing at the University of Virginia, in an article he coauthored in the *Journal of Business Ethics* called "Choose, Choose, Choose, Choose, Choose, Choose, Choose: Emerging and Prospective Research on the Deleterious Effects of Living in Consumer Hyperchoice."

> *"The ideology of consumption and the imperative of consumer choice have washed across the globe," writes Mr. Mick. "In today's developed economies there is an increasing amount of buying, amidst an ever-increasing amount of purchase options, amidst an ever-increasing amount of stress, amidst an ever-decreasing amount of discretionary time."*

The result is not a wonderful feeling of power, but confusion and regret. Hyperchoice is "initially attractive but ultimately unsatisfying," he says, adding that "hyperchoice is psychologically draining."

 JUST SAYING NO

People will only pay partial attention, even when the communication is something they're interested in.

The M&Ms diet . . .

So much stuff, so little substance: Information has become like junk food. All those words and data are the M&Ms of communication—so many brightly colored pieces of sugar, with absolutely no nutritional value. You can easily pop M&Ms into your mouth, one after another (and another), and not even think about what you're doing. You may choose a red one over a green one, but you can't really taste the difference. And although eating a bag may cause an immediate sugar rush, what comes later is a headache that just won't quit.

3. Information anxiety

In his 1989 book *Information Anxiety*, the architect, designer, and information guru Richard Saul Wurman coined the term—and in the 2 decades since the anxiety has only grown along with the surfeit of information.

As Mr. Wurman writes, "Most of us are growing apprehensive about our seeming inability to deal with, understand, manipulate, or comprehend the epidemic of data that increasingly dominates our lives.

"Where once, during the age of industry, the world was ruled by natural resources, it is now run on information, and while resources are finite, information seems to be infinite."

The symptoms of this condition are as numerous as the data that causes it. "It can be experienced as moments of frustration with a manual that refuses to divulge the secret to operating a video recorder," writes Mr. Wurman. "It can also be manifested as a chronic malaise, a pervasive fear

◀◀ The symptoms of this condition are as numerous as the data that causes it.

"In our compulsive drive for more, we are making ourselves sick."

Dr. Peter C. Whybrow,
director of the Semel Institute of
Neuroscience and Human Behavior
at the University of California,
Los Angeles

that we are about to be overwhelmed by the very material we need to master in order to function in this world."

4. Attention deficit trait

If information anxiety is troubling, attention deficit trait (ADT) is disabling. The term ADT has been coined by psychiatrist Edward M. Hallowell, M.D., to describe a condition caused by brain overload. "The core symptoms are distractibility, inner frenzy, and impatience," writes Dr. Hallowell in an article in the January 2005 issue of the *Harvard Business Review*, "Overloaded Circuits: Why Smart People Underperform."

"People with ADT have difficulty staying organized, setting priorities, and managing time," Dr. Hallowell adds.

What sets ADT apart from ADHD (attention deficit/hyperactivity disorder), a neurological disorder that has a genetic component, according to Dr. Hallowell, is that "ADT springs entirely from the environment. Like the traffic jam, ADT is an artifact of modern life. It is brought on by the demands on our time and attention that have exploded over the past two decades. As our minds fill with noise—feckless synaptic events signifying nothing—the brain gradually loses its capacity to attend fully and thoroughly to anything."

5. ADHD

The only attention syndrome that's been officially recognized by the American Psychiatric Association is attention deficit/hyperactivity disorder, or ADHD (which used to be known as ADD). What's fascinating is how many adults—people in your target audience—may

 **JUST SAYING NO**

People will throw out more than half the paper mail with no more than a quick glance—or leave it in a pile to get to when they have time. (Six months later, when they can't stand the mess anymore, it will all get thrown into the recycling bin.)

suffer from this disorder. The exact number of people with ADHD is not known, but one estimate is that 4.3 percent of the U.S. adult population—more than 8 million Americans—is affected.

ADHD, which has neurobiological origins, manifests itself as a persistent pattern of inattention and/or hyperactivity-impulsivity. Not surprisingly, according to a 2005 study, "Capturing America's Attention," which was presented at the American Psychiatric Association annual meeting, people with ADHD find it difficult to cope with the demands of everyday life.

The attention deficient bottom line

Although we hope that you yourself are serene, centered, and free of stress, we know that your audience is none of the above. They're either informally stressed-out or clinically so. The last thing they want is more useless information. What they need is someone who understands their pain and communicates with them in a way that actually helps.

What has to change: The way you communicate

Even if you haven't read every word of this chapter, by now you get it. There is no longer a guarantee that just because you say/write/broadcast/or put it on a Web site, it will be heard or read.

Before you can get your message across, your audience needs to be paying attention. To get their attention, you will need to make bold changes that cut through the clutter.

ADHD FACTS

Forty-six percent of adults with ADHD have a hard time paying attention at work (compared to 20% without ADHD). And 24% of adults with ADHD experience symptoms that prevent normal activities, such as work, for an average of 11 days every month (compared to 9% who don't have the disorder).

INSIGHT 1:
The novel vs. NASCAR

If we could convince people who communicate to do just one thing differently, it would be this: Stop writing as if your audience has unlimited time and attention.

That may seem kind of funny, coming from us (the writers), but let us explain: In a world that's information-overloaded and starved for time and attention, people's willingness to read long prose is declining rapidly.

And yet every day we see communicators engage in egregious acts of writing excess: The 600-word intranet

◀◀ Stop writing as if your audience has unlimited time and attention.

Our epiphany . . .

When we began thinking about the challenge of capturing people's attention, we naturally applied our own perspective and experience. "We're just as busy as anyone else," we said, "But we haven't tuned out and stopped paying attention." In fact, we were consuming more than ever: Digesting three newspapers a day. Avidly reading online newsletters. Carrying a shoulder bag full of reading material onto planes and into doctor's offices. Dreaming about our next vacation, when we could do nothing but sit on a beach and read.

It was that last part, the part about the beach and a book, that made us realize that we're not like most of the people we need to communicate with. Our idea of heaven is to be someplace where we can read in peace. Most people dream of being someplace where they can escape the onslaught of words. In order to be successful, we knew we'd have to take a dramatically different approach to communicating—an approach that deals with the reality of our audience's needs.

This book models this new approach. Read on to learn more.

entry. The 1,000-word promotional e-mail. The 1,500-word newsletter article.

If these missives seem too long to us, avid readers who communicate for a living, imagine how harried audience members must react: "I'll just skim this," "Maybe I'll get to it later," "Forget it; I'm too busy."

Here's the hard reality: For an increasing number of people these days, reading is an obligation, not an avocation.

Today, less than half of adult Americans read literature. ▶▶

For proof, consider these facts from the 2004 study from The National Endowment for the Arts, "Reading At Risk":

- The percentage of adult Americans reading literature has dropped dramatically—by 19 percent—over the past 20 years.
- Today, less than half of adult Americans read literature (46.7 percent, or 96 million people).
- Literary reading is declining among all age groups (including a 12.3 percent drop for those 35–44) with the steepest decline among those 18–24. (–28 percent)

Contrast this with the rapid rise of NASCAR (The National Association for Stock Car Racing):

- In 2004, 75 million Americans—one-third of the U.S. adult population—were NASCAR fans, up 19 percent from 1995.
- NASCAR is the #1 spectator sport, with 17 of the top 20 attended events in the United States (Attendance increased 28 percent over the past decade.)

66 The only way to communicate is to understand what it is like not to understand. **99**

Richard Saul Wurman

- The Daytona 500 Race, NASCAR's biggest, got a 10.9 rating (percentage of the 109.6 million TV homes in the United States) when it was broadcast on the Fox network in 2005 (a 40 percent rise since 1995). That means about 1 out of 9 Americans was watching.

Although literature still has the lead, at this rate NASCAR will overtake novels on the next lap.

But we know what you're thinking: Don't people who watch NASCAR also read novels? And vice versa? Sure, but you can imagine the Friday night conversations across America:

> *"Wow, it's been a long week. Let's do something fun this weekend—you know, kick back, relax, let loose."*

> *"Great idea, honey. What do you have in mind?"*

> *"I know: Let's get really crazy and tackle* **Anna Karenina.***"*

Not likely. Our point is simple: Your audience members are the same people who are rejecting reading literature as a leisure-time activity. Instead, they're loading the kids in the RV, putting on their Jeff Gordon caps, and driving out to the speedway.

Until your communication vehicle is a racecar, better put the brakes on your literary ambitions.

Your audience members are the same people who are rejecting reading literature as a leisure-time activity. ▶▶

Section 2
A Compelling Strategy for Getting Attention

2 | Focus on "you"

In this chapter, you'll learn about the most effective strategy for grabbing people's attention: Focusing your communication on their needs, not yours.

MOST OF US HAVE been unlucky enough to have gone out on a date with someone who looks great on paper, but who turns out to be a narcissistic jerk. The guy (we flipped a coin to choose the gender) finds himself fascinating. He laughs before he delivers a joke's punch line—that's how funny he thinks he is. When you get a word in edgewise, you get the feeling he's not listening—just waiting for you to stop talking so he can start again. Whatever his age, he's the poster child for the "Me Generation." The date seems to go on forever. You're convinced you've slipped through a tear in the fabric of the universe where time stands still. You can't wait for the evening to be over.

Contrast this with the experience of meeting someone who takes a genuine interest in you. This encounter could be romantic or platonic—the person could be a date, or a friend, or teacher. The point is that he finds you fascinating. He listens to you. He cares about what you say. He laughs at your jokes. You enjoy his company. The difference between scenario A and scenario B is obvious. In the first instance, it's all about him; in the second, you truly matter.

◀◀ He listens to you. He cares about what you say. He laughs at your jokes. You enjoy his company.

If B is so much better than A, why is so much written communication like the bad date instead of like the rewarding relationship? **Because people design communication that is totally focused on what they want to say and ignores what the audience wants to hear!**

We don't know for sure why people, including many highly paid professional communicators, dismiss the hand that feeds them their $4 chai tea lattes, but we can have a couple of guesses:

1. It's easier.
2. It's familiar.

Trying to figure out what your audience wants, and then delivering it, is a lot of work. ▶▶

Let's deal with easier first. If you are writing to satisfy your needs, there is not a whole lot of work to do. You know what you like. On the other hand, as we'll discuss in Chapter 3, trying to figure out what your audience wants, and then delivering it, is a lot of work. You've got to put on their shoes and walk around in them. However, you think your audience's Jimmy Choo shoes are ugly and impractical. The heels are really high. They hurt your feet. You whine, "Can't I just wear my Keds instead?" We say, get over it. The fact is, the key principle of getting and holding attention is to focus on the audience—to help *your* audience solve a problem, meet a need, and answer a question.

Get inspired by reading magazines

The people who really get this concept of writing for their audience—and who do it well—are those who run service magazines such as *Better Homes and Gardens, Bon Appétit, Seventeen*, and *Men's Health*.

These publications are literally built on the philosophy of service: To "serve" readers. The purpose of every single article is to help readers do something better—be happier, thinner, have a nicer house and better-behaved children,

Your mantra should be:

" It's not about me;

it's all about you. "

improve their golf game or lower their heart rate, meet the perfect mate, or find the ideal doctor.

And, lest you scoff at magazines for being inconsequential, consider this: 84 percent of adults aged 18 and over read magazines regularly—compared to the less than 50 percent who read novels. There are more than 7,000 magazines published in North America, and in 2004, 480 new magazines were introduced.

As Jean LemMon, former editor of *Better Homes and Gardens* describes it, "Service journalism . . . goes beyond the delivery of pure information." It is "action journalism. As such, it must include inspiration for the reader to want to do something, and then the editorial backup that equips the reader to actually go ahead and do it."

First and foremost in service journalism, says Ms. LemMon, the focus is on readers. In other words, it's all about them—not about the publishers, editors, or writers.

To understand the appeal, go to any newsstand and pick up a copy. Even before you open the magazine, you'll see by the cover that the focus is on the reader:

- "Feeling blue? How to know if you're in danger"
- "What to wear now . . . and into fall"
- "Your best marathon! Train less, run faster"
- "Are standardized tests good for your child?"
- "127 top travel agents and what they can do for you"
- "Get smart, slim, and satisfied"

In every single case, the focus is on the potential reader—not on the writer. What is the intriguing thing

⚠ A FEW GOOD SERVICE MAGAZINES

Allure
American Angler
Bike
Bride's
Child
Family Circle
Fitness
Good Housekeeping
Money
Popular Mechanics
Prevention
Real Simple
Self

Can you pass the refrigerator test?

What should you be aiming for as you set off to create service journalism? Don Ranly, acclaimed professor at the University of Missouri School of Journalism, knows. According to Mr. Ranly, the ideal that any communicator should strive for is what he calls "refrigerator journalism": information that your audience will find so pertinent that they will cut it out and stick it on their refrigerators or bulletin boards. "In today's microwave world," he says, "in-a-hurry readers want practical information" that they can put to use immediately.

about the list in the sidebar to the left? It doesn't matter who the audience is, fishermen (*American Angler*), women who are about to be married (*Bride's*) or the middle class wondering how to make ends meet (*Money*), the (incredibly sharp) focus is always on the reader.

Magazine editors feel so passionately about the idea that "it's all about you" that they've even created publications that have "you" or "me" right in the title. In doing so, publishers are trying to create a sense that their magazines are geared to their readers' individual needs. Eric Heuvel, media director of advertising firm Citigate, summed up the trend as follows:

> *"I think a lot of what you are seeing is the influence of the Internet." Naming publications "for you," Mr. Heuvel explains, "is a way of trying to connect with consumers."*

◀◀ Publishers are trying to create a sense that their magazines are geared to their readers' individual needs.

How to headline

The two most compelling headlines on magazine covers—the ones editors use to attract browsers and sell copies—are "you" and "how to." Both speak directly to readers to offer them the promise of solving a problem or achieving a goal. Using the words "you" and "how to" shows the focus is clearly on them.

*Provide informa-
tion that's acces-
sible, friendly,
and relevant.* ▶▶

That's certainly the case of *All You*, a Time Inc. publication that's sold only in Wal-Mart (which is not only the world's biggest retailer, but is also responsible for 15 percent of all magazine newsstand sales nationwide). *All You* is designed to meet the needs of a very specific demographic: women from Middle America who shop in discount stores and who seek practical, down-to-earth information.

For Me, a lifestyle magazine from the publisher of *Woman's Day*, Hachette Filipacchi, has a different demographic—women between the ages of 25 and 35. But the intent is similar: to provide information that's accessible, friendly, and relevant.

Putting this strategy to work

If you don't work in magazine publishing, how do you apply these principles to your own communication? Let's take a close look at what **not** to do, using a real-life example (*see following page*). Employees working in the headquarters of a very large, well-known company a couple of years ago opened their e-mail to find the following message.

HQ DEVELOPMENT HELPS EMPLOYEES BUILD CORE CAPABILITIES

I am pleased to share with you information about the Headquarters Development team and the important learning opportunities it provides. The HQ Development team is comprised of performance consultants who helped identify the key capabilities employees must possess to support the organization's goals and then designed a curriculum to help employees develop those capabilities.

The team's key areas of focus are:

Orientation—helping new employees get acclimated by teaching them about the organization's business, goals, and success factors.

Core capabilities—providing learning resources to help employees at all levels build the skills, actions, and behaviors they need to succeed in the company.

Leadership—identifying the requirements for leaders within the company and implementing development opportunities for them.

HQ Development hosts a full curriculum of classroom-based learning resources. However, since we recognize that different individuals prefer to learn in different ways, we will add other learning resources, such as mentoring programs, e-learning, and self-directed study later this year.

Headquarters Development is part of the field force organization and reports into Global Learning & Development. The group partners closely with Human Resources, Open Enrollment, and Consulting Services in order to provide employees with seamless learning and development support.

Our team consists of:

Jerry, VP, Global L&D
Sarah, Director/Team Leader
Leslie, Director
Lorelei, Senior Manager
Caroline, Coordinator

Jennifer, Sr. Director/Team Leader
Ryan, Director/Team Leader
Jerralyn, Director
Eleanor, Manager
Esmerelda, Admin. Assistant

HQ Development is preparing to launch a new intranet site called *Your Site For Development* that will replace the New Horizons in Open Enrollment site. The new site will serve as a directory to the many learning resources we've developed, helping you focus on the capabilities you need to succeed in the company's matrix organization. We will provide you with further information about the site once it is launched.

For more information, feel free to call any team member. We look forward to helping you develop the skills, knowledge, and behaviors that will help the company reach its business goals.

ZZZZ. Oh, sorry, we nodded off there for a moment.

There's nothing technically wrong with the writing. (Granted, it is very dull and very corporate, but the gram-mar's okay and if you actually managed to read all the way through, you saw that all the words were spelled correctly.)

The fundamental problem with this announcement is the focus: It's completely about the folks writing the mes-sage, not the people reading it. Although the subject line is somewhat promising, the e-mail quickly degrades into a puff piece about HQ Development and its "important" work.

This might be okay to send to team members' parents ("Mom! Look what I did!") or their alumni magazines ("See, I told you I would amount to something"), but it doesn't work to grab the attention of its intended audience: employees in headquarters who would participate in learn-ing and development.

How would we do it differently? First, we'd wait until the intranet site was ready to be announced—otherwise, what's the purpose of the communication?—and then we'd change the focus 180 degrees, so that it's all about the employee (*see following page*).

What to do differently

✓ Focus on what your audience needs and wants to know. (That means leaving your own ego at the door.)

✓ Provide enough information to make your communication useful, but not so much that you overwhelm the audience.

NEW DEVELOPMENT SERVICES HELP YOU DEVELOP KEY SKILLS

A new intranet site—*Your Site for Development*—has been launched to provide headquarters employees with the resources you need to build your development plan and choose training to support it.

The site, which replaces the *New Horizons in Open Enrollment* site, is one aspect of the services offered by the HQ Development team. The team's mission is to design training for current and new employees to give them key capabilities to support the company's goals.

Visit the Web site for learning options

The cornerstone of HQ Development's learning program is a full curriculum of classroom-based courses. However, since different individuals prefer to learn in different ways, later this year we will add other learning resources, such as mentoring programs, e-learning, and self-directed study. We'll update the intranet site as these programs are developed.

Contact team members to find out more

If you have questions or need additional information, please feel free to contact any team member:

Jerry, VP, Global L&D	Jennifer, Sr. Director/Team Leader
Sarah, Director/Team Leader	Ryan, Director/Team Leader
Leslie, Director	Jerralyn, Director
Lorelei, Senior Manager	Eleanor, Manager
Caroline, Coordinator	Esmerelda, Admin. Assistant

We look forward to providing you with the skills and knowledge to help you succeed.

 INSIGHT 2:
The end of the beginning

Here's a cautionary tale from the halls of academia—well, maybe not academia, but high school. We recently had the privilege of attending a high school graduation ceremony that demonstrated the dangers of the "me, me, me" approach to communication.

Ceremonies (dedications, anniversaries, and, of course, graduations) are inherently tricky because speakers naturally want to be memorable and appear wise. So it's all too easy to venture into dangerous territory: the Pit of Sanctimony, the Canyon of Clichés, or the Abyss of Officious Quotations.

In the case of this graduation, we were guaranteed to take a fall: There were 16 speakers. (We're not kidding: 16

Getting started

How can you put "all about you" into practice? The rest of this book is devoted to specific tactics and strategies that answer that question, but here are some ways to get started:

Old way	New way
Me, me, me	All about you
Share what I want to say	Convey what you want to hear
List all the attributes of what I'm communicating	Focus on the benefits to you
Give the whole story	Cut out everything but what matters to you most
Make the tone sound official and important	Be friendly and personal; chatty and colloquial

by actual count.) That meant the ceremony went on for more than 2 hours, until our derrieres were sore, our brains were fried, and our bladders were bursting.

It also meant 16 recollections of "when we were younger" or "highlights from childhood/high school/last week." And 16 pieces of advice on how to be (a) happy, (b) successful, (c) kind to others, or (d) all of the above. And 16 sets of quotations from famous literary or historical figures, including William James, Henry James, F. Scott Fitzgerald, and Gandhi.

The most popular quotation was from Sir Winston Churchill. (You know, the British politician and prime minister, who lived from 1874 to 1965). No fewer than 3 speakers used the same Churchill remark: "Now this is not the end. It is not even the beginning of the end. But it is, perhaps, the end of the beginning."

It's probably not surprising that 3 people wrote the Churchill quotation into their speeches. But it was amazing

---

What Churchill wanted to say

A quick Google search yields Churchill quotes that are:

✔ **More graduation-appropriate:** "History will be kind to me for I intend to write it."

✔ **More provocative:** "Personally I'm always ready to learn, although I do not always like being taught."

✔ **And a lot funnier:** "From now on, ending a sentence with a preposition is something up with which I will not put."

to us in the audience that after the first speaker used the quotation, the other 2 didn't change their remarks: They just went ahead and said "beginning of the end, end of the beginning" as planned. Why?

Because the other speakers weren't listening.

No one was, really—certainly not the seniors, who were thinking about the party afterward. Not the parents, who were waiting for their child's name to be called. Not the rest of the audience, or the band, or the chorus, or the pretty little birds up there in the tree, framed against the fading light of the summer evening sky.

If the speeches had really been for any of us, they would have been short.

They would have been free of rhetoric, quotations, or literary references. They would have been intensely personal, the way these kids actually speak to one another: "I'm proud of you, and of me. At times it's been hard, but we've had some great times. I'm ready to go, but I'll miss you."

That would have been meaningful. And if anyone had done that, we would have cried real tears, tears of joy, not tears of relief when the ceremony finally, finally came to an end.

3 | Love your audience

"KNOW YOUR AUDIENCE" is one of the oldest tenets of communication. The concept, of course, is that the better you understand the demographic profile, needs, and preferences of the people you're trying to reach, the better you can design communication that will get through to them.

It's certainly a sound principle—one which we will explore in just a second—but we don't believe the idea of knowing your audience goes far enough. In order to break through today's noise and nonsense, you have to go well beyond knowledge: You have to love your audience.

Like Tina Turner, you may well ask, "What's love got to do with it?" We'll show you what we mean in just a few pages, but in the meantime, remember this: If you feel separate from—or worse, superior to—the people you're trying to communicate with, you'll never be effective at engaging them. You've got to sit right down at your audience's messy table and order yourself (and them) a beer.

Stay with us (the beer's good and cold) and we'll explain.

Getting to know you

In the good old days (or the dark ages, depending on how you look at them), connecting with your audience was easier because you had so much in common with them. There

> In Chapter 2, we emphasized how critical it is to focus on your audience. (It's not about you; it's about them.) Once you've achieved that focus, you need to really get to know your audience—in fact, you've got to get close enough to love them. Doing so helps you create communication that gets your audience's attention because it meets their needs.

66 **People only understand things in terms of their experience, which means that you must get within their experience. 99**

**Rules for Radicals:
A Pragmatic Primer for
Realistic Radicals—
*Saul D. Alinsky***

was less societal diversity. The work force was much more homogenous. Customers could be categorized into one unified segment—the mass market—or just a few subsegments—middle class, rich, and poor. Most communication was fairly "local"—targeted to a specific region or country.

Today, it's a brand-new ball game. Whichever audience you target—colleagues, customers, or other stakeholders—its members are likely to be very different from you, in terms of background, education, interests, geography, even primary language. You're no longer looking into a mirror—you're gazing out a window onto a crowded square that resembles a street festival and sounds like the Tower of Babel.

How different are they?

Members of 4 racial and ethnic minorities make up more than half the population in Hawaii (77 percent), New Mexico (56.5 percent), California (55.5 percent) and Texas (50.2 percent), according to the U.S. Census Bureau (2004).

From 2000 to 2004, according to the Census Bureau, the total population of the United States grew by 4.3 percent. Yet the African-American population rose 5.7 percent, the Asian population increased 16.2 percent, and the Hispanic population grew by 17 percent. It just isn't a cliché to say the country is becoming more diverse; it's a fact.

Women's participation in the work force has increased at an extraordinarily rapid pace. In 1950, according to the U.S. Bureau of Labor Statistics, 34 percent of women aged 16 or older were in the labor force; by 2002, the rate had increased to 60 percent, and by 2010, it's expected to reach 62 percent. The percentage of the total work force that is female has grown proportionately: By 2010, nearly half (48 percent) of all U.S. workers will be women.

What this means is that you can't assume that communication content or style that appeals to you will necessarily appeal to your target audience. As you saw in Chapter 1, just the fact that you're reading this book puts you in the minority. Chances are good that the people you're communicating with are less interested in reading and writing than you are.

CEOs are different

One obstacle that many of us face in creating communication that appeals to our audience is the fact that our first "audience" is our boss—and often the most important "client" we have is senior management, the people who often have to sign off on what we have to say—and of course, sign our paychecks. But CEOs—and other senior executives—are even more different from the intended audience than we are. In fact, CEOs experience the world completely differently than everyone else, according to Russell L. Ackoff, coauthor of *Beating the System: Using Creativity to Outsmart Bureaucracies.*

Our first "audience" is our boss. ▶▶

In an interview in *Across the Board* magazine, Mr. Ackoff points out that CEOs "don't experience the same problems that you and I do. As an ordinary consumer, sometimes you don't know whom to call to get a problem fixed. You call and get a prepackaged message from some synthetic voice that gives you 10 alternatives, none of which cover your question. And you're left either hanging, puzzled, or trying all kinds of nonsense."

However, Mr. Ackoff explains, "if you're the CEO of a large corporation, you know the CEOs of other large corporations. If you get abused by the system, you pick up the phone and call a friend [your fellow CEO], and you get your problem fixed."

Demographic data

Interested in learning more about demographics and how they shape perspectives and attitudes? There is lots of fascinating information available on the Internet. More importantly, these Web sites provide a variety of data, allowing you to take a close look at your target audience.

United States demographics
Bureau of Labor Statistics: *www.bls.gov*
Census Bureau: *www.census.gov*
Department of Labor: *www.dol.gov*

Global demographics
UNESCO: *www.unesco.org*
World Economic Forum: *www.weforum.org*
The World Factbook: *www.cia.gov/cia/publications/factbook*

What's true in customer service is true in communication. When a CEO reads something and asks, "What does this mean?" someone is there to provide an answer—or get it fast.

Senior leaders aren't out there in the world like the rest of us, wondering, "How does this affect me? What should I do differently?" and finding out that no one has the answers.

What can you do about the fact that CEOs have a completely unique—and skewed—communication experience? Well, you can hope that they take Mr. Ackoff's suggestion that "top management place themselves in the position of the customer, like a CEO of an airline flying in coach."

But if your CEO won't spend his day replicating the communication experience of employees, customers, or other audiences, you need to bring the experience to the CEO. Make sure you have both accurate data and compelling qualitative feedback to bring the audience's experience to life.

Helping CEOs (and senior managers) see the light

Here's an example of providing CEOs with the information they need to see things from the audience's point of view. Alison was working with a major health care firm that had recently invested heavily in technology to allow any employee with a computer to see a Webcast or video clip of the CEO speaking; they could then make comments or ask questions online.

As a result, the CEO felt that he no longer had to visit manufacturing plants and other remote locations to conduct "town hall meetings" with employees—if everyone in the company could see him remotely and ask questions, why take all the time and expense to travel?

But manufacturing employees and those in transportation didn't have easy access to technology. As a matter of fact, these employees could only use centrally located computer "kiosks" during breaks or after their shifts were over, when the computers were usually occupied by people checking their electronic pay stubs or looking up a benefits question.

Alison knew that the CEO needed to be shown the light, so he could visualize the way communication actually worked for employees. She worked with her client to compile data on employees' computer access (such as the number of employees per computer, how many minutes of access they had, what they used computers for, and so on). She also conducted focus groups to learn what they thought about computer video broadcasts versus CEO-hosted town hall meetings.

Employees said things like this: "When the CEO comes to visit, I feel like he really cares about us and the work we're doing." "The CEO is candid when he answers questions face-to-face. When you type a question in the computer, the answer comes back very packaged." "Our production goals are very ambitious, and I work really hard during my shift. By the time it's over, I'm exhausted, and the last thing I want to do is wait in line to use the kiosk."

 The feedback worked, and the CEO agreed to resume his town hall meetings. The most interesting part of this exercise to us was that, although the CEO certainly took the data seriously, what he found most compelling were the employee verbatim quotes. Why? Because those quotes seemed real and immediate to him—he could imagine employees making those suggestions directly to him, and he thus felt the need to respond.

What you need to know

Who are your audience members and what do they care about? Obviously, you may need to do a little investigation to find out. We won't provide a treatise on demographic or market research here—there are scores of journals and books available (we have listed a few in the sidebar on page 41) and dozens of firms that specialize in research. And, since we're pragmatists, we're not even going to suggest that you must collect mounds of data to analyze your audience.

Our recommendation is that you at least find out the answers to 5 essential questions about the people you're trying to communicate with:

1. Where are they? (Are they concentrated in one region? One country? Or spread out across the globe?)
2. How old are they? (Most demographers believe, correctly, that age or age range is a key indicator of experience and attitude. An approach that works for 20-somethings probably won't resonate with people old enough to be their grandparents.)
3. What is their occupation? Do they have specialized skills you need to take into account; are you communicating with senior management or the rank and file?
4. How do they spend their work days?
5. What do they care about (that relates to what you're trying to communicate)?

Something about Mary

If you do your clothes shopping on Madison Avenue or Rodeo Drive, you've probably never heard of the specialty retailer Christopher & Banks. But this 463-store clothing

◀◀ Find out the answers to 5 essential questions.

chain has made "know your audience" its key strategy, resulting in rapid expansion and consistent sales growth.

Because this audience profile is so integral to every decision, Christopher & Banks has created a persona for its core customer: Mary. She's is a 48-year-old mother of 2 who does not want to dress like she's 25. Mary lives in a small town or suburbia. She likes clothing that matches: sweaters that go perfectly with pants, shirts that go with jackets. And she is old-fashioned enough to find corny designs—embroidered motifs, gingham, ruffles—appealing.

According to the *Wall Street Journal*, Mary came to life when then company president William Prange (now chairman and CEO) heard a speech in the mid-1990s by an executive at The Limited, who said that understanding a customer's lifestyle is essential to knowing what the customer wants to wear.

Christopher & Banks then conducted focus groups with its target audience—women aged 35 to 55—and developed the profile of Mary. This profile is more than a sketch—it's a detailed portrait/character analysis:

- Mary works as a teacher, nurse, or bank teller.
- She drives a minivan.
- She likes casual sit-down chain restaurants (like T.G.I. Friday's), not fast food.
- Her favorite magazines are *People* and *Good Housekeeping*.

By creating the character of Mary, Christopher & Banks "created a person and devised a company to fill her closet," says CEO William Prange. Mary is so central to how Christopher & Banks makes decisions that the company has chosen a photograph of a woman to personify the character. "In the current photo, Mary has wavy, shoulder-length chestnut hair and some lines around her eyes and mouth, though she looks younger than 48," according to the *Wall Street Journal*. Periodically, the company shows the photo, and those of other women, to focus groups to decide which one best represents Mary.

All about Bob

We found the Christopher & Banks approach to getting to know your audience so compelling that we've applied it many times in our own work. What makes it such an effective tool is that the emphasis is not on abstract data—"53 percent of our customers drive minivans"—but on the specific character details that bring an audience to life and help you connect with its needs.

More about market research

Michael B. Rynowecer, president of The BTI Consulting Group, a market research firm based in Boston, recommends the following 3 books to help you understand the basics of what he does for a living:

✓ *The Market Research Toolbox: A Concise Guide for Beginners,* by Edward F. McQuarrie, Sage Publications, 2005

✓ *Market Research: A Guide to Planning, Methodology, and Evaluation,* by Paul N. Hague, Kogan Page, 2002

✓ *Business to Business Marketing Research: Understanding and Measuring Business Markets,* by Ruth McNeil, Kogan Page, 2005

For example, people in corporate headquarters often have a very vague idea about what "real life" is like for employees of the rest of the company: They really think that everyone who works for the company wears expensive suits, walks on plush carpet, eats in a restaurant-quality cafeteria, and parks their car in covered parking.

To deliver a dose of reality, we took feedback from focus groups and other employee research to create a profile of a "typical" employee—someone who's out there sweating and doing real work (not this frou-frou intellectual stuff).

That's how we created Bob, a factory employee at a consumer products company. Ever since he graduated from technical school 17 years ago, Bob has worked at the company's manufacturing facility in Oklahoma; his dad also worked for the company, so Bob has deep roots in the organization. Bob is proud of the job he does, but he doesn't feel that his work defines him. He is a big fan of NASCAR, and every year he goes to Texas on a duck-hunting trip with his buddies. Bob uses technology in his job, and his kids have a computer at home, but he doesn't really like computers.

> Your target customer is not a demographic with a checkbook. ▶▶

This type of profile is also useful when creating sales/marketing strategies on customers. Your target customer is not a demographic with a checkbook: He or she is a person with real needs and concerns. By creating a character sketch of your intended audience you'll connect with them more effectively.

From knowledge to love

Christopher & Banks has clearly gone beyond gathering data about its customers: The company has created the character of Mary to achieve a deeper state of understanding that translates into a personal relationship. As Kathryn

The competitive advantage

"You need a killer application . . . a new idea . . . that establishes a new category in its field . . . What is that application? Simply put: Love is the killer app. Those of us who use love as a point of differentiation in business will separate ourselves from our competitors just as world-class distance runners separate themselves from the rest of the pack trailing behind them."

—Tim Sanders, Yahoo! leadership coach and author of *Love Is the Killer App*

Gangstee, head of merchandising for the chain, says of Mary, "We like her. She's a good person. A good wife, a good mother. She's someone you'd want to sit down and have lunch with."

Sounds like love to us. The idea is that, even though Mary (and our character Bob) may be very different than you are—with a different lifestyle, interests, even values—if you love your audience members unreservedly, you'll be successful in connecting with them.

"Never forget that every customer and prospective customer of yours is a human being—an organic, intelligent individual with a constantly evolving set of attitudes and opinions," write Don Peppers and Martha Rogers in their book *The One to One Future*. "Stop thinking in terms of audiences and faceless masses of eyes and ears. Think, instead, of human beings—individual human beings."

Show me the love!
Your love has to be real—not manufactured or manipulative—and unconditional. You have to clearly see your

audience members' faults but love them anyway. Your love has to be unwavering, despite your audience's inattention, inconstancy, and even infidelity.

Only by truly loving your audience can you communicate in a way that's truly about them, not about you. The leap to loving brings you in touch with what matters to people. Suddenly you're able to communicate in ways that profoundly connect. You're not on the other side of the chasm from your audience members: You're right there next to them, talking softly, saying what they've always wanted to hear.

Think of those who are brilliant at honoring, respecting, and, yes, loving the people they're trying to get through to:

- *Procter & Gamble.* P&G's marketing not only elevates the product—cleaning a floor is important—it also takes the consumer's needs seriously. P&G never talks down to its consumers. The tone is always supportive, no matter how humble the topic. As P&G Chief Marketing Officer Jim Stengel puts it, "We have created a

What to do differently

✔ Get to know your audience—individually, not just as a group. Create a character sketch. Do focus groups. Read the written answers on marketing surveys. You won't connect with your audience if you only see them as a bunch of statistics. (Hey, would you go out with someone who only judged you on your measurements?)

✔ Find out what your audience really cares about.

✔ Accept your audience for who they are—warts and all—and communicate based on unconditional love.

mantra of sorts in putting the consumer at the center of all we do. This is not something new for our company, as we've had a strong consumer focus for more than 165 years." But recently P&G has taken this focus to new levels. "Consumer-centric has no assumptions," says Mr. Stengel. It begins by identifying your customer, determining what is unique about him or her, and then meeting them where they are. "We engage consumers at times and places that are important in their lives and reach out to them on their terms," he adds.

- *Consumer magazines—especially women's magazines.* We talked about these publications in Chapter 2, and here they are again—remember that "service magazines" seek to provide the reader with information that will serve her needs. Again, there's nothing patronizing about these publications—they're friendly and helpful. Look at the cover lines of a recent issue of *Family Circle*: "Delicious No-Cook Dinners," "14 Medical Tests That Can Save Your Life," "12 Ways to Be a Gutsy Woman."

- *Great preachers.* We're not regular churchgoers ourselves, but we can certainly appreciate the way great preachers start with the idea that even sinners are loved by God—and by the preacher himself. How compelling is that?

All this talk about love, and we can just picture you squirming in your chair. But the "love your audience" concept is pragmatic as well as philosophical. Far too often, we see communication that's so attuned to the needs of CEOs (or someone's immediate boss) that it is unintentionally disrespectful of the intended audience.

◀◀ There's nothing patronizing about these publications—they're friendly and helpful.

SHOW ME THE LOVE:
DISRESPECTFUL COMMUNICATION

Example	Problem
Jargon, acronyms, technical terms, or corporate speak	Seems like a secret language that the audience doesn't understand
Using communication channels, especially technology, that audience members aren't comfortable with	Makes people feel dumb
Communication that's linear or that only allows one choice for navigation	Does not allow audience members to control the experience on their own terms
Static, one-way communication	Gives people the sense they're being "talked to" with no way to participate, interact, or give feedback

You can't change everything, but we believe that if you lead with love, the rest will follow.

➡ INSIGHT 3:
People who love Lawrence Welk

There, tucked among the obituaries on July 25, 2005, was a notice that Myron Floren had died. Don't remember Myron? He was Lawrence Welk's accordionist and sidekick.

If you're young, sophisticated, or both, Lawrence Welk's name may not even be familiar to you. But Alison vividly remembers Mr. Welk and his television show that ran on Saturday nights on ABC from 1955 to 1971.

Alison's grandfather, who was an amateur trumpet player, loved old-fashioned music. So when she went to

66Keep it simple so the audience can feel like they can do it, too. You have to play what the people will understand.**99**

Lawrence Welk

visit her grandparents for Saturday-night sleepovers, Alison and her grandparents had a little ritual: They'd eat dinner or snacks on TV tables in the living room and watch every minute of *The Lawrence Welk Show*.

Mr. Welk referred to the format as "champagne music": easy-listening, old-fashioned ballroom tunes delivered by his "family" of wholesome musicians, singers, and dancers. (To add to the "champagne" effect, every show featured a very active bubble machine.) The format was the opposite of cutting edge; it was designed to be safe, familiar, and homey.

Mr. Welk himself seemed very modest and approachable . . . even a little ridiculous. He was born in North Dakota (in 1903) to Alsatian parents in a German-speaking farm community; after dropping out of school in the 4th grade, Mr. Welk spoke no English until he was 21. And he had a thick accent and a stiff stage manner that was often imitated by comedians in his day.

But there was nothing funny about Mr. Welk's ability to understand what his viewers wanted. When ABC cancelled the show in 1971 because it was "too old," Mr. Welk lined up 200 independent stations to create his own syndication network. The show was produced and ran for 11 more years.

If you happen to catch *The Lawrence Welk Show* today, you'll no doubt think it's corny. And it would be easy to dismiss fans of the genre as out of touch. But it's possible that someone you want to reach is a secret (or out-of-the-closet) Lawrence Welk devotee. You don't have to love the music. But to be successful at communication, you need to love the audience.

⚠ STILL POPULAR

In 1987, reruns of the *Lawrence Welk Show* began appearing—they're still shown on many public television stations, where the show has the highest ratings of any syndicated program, reaching 3 million households every week. Three million viewers, even today! And that doesn't even count: the reunion television specials that are made every so often, the Welk live shows in Branson, Missouri, and on the road, or the 3 Welk Resorts, in San Diego, Branson, and Palm Springs.

Section 3
Techniques to Grab and Hold People's Attention

4 | Create a high concept

Even if you really know and love your audience, you just have a few seconds to grab their attention. In this chapter, you'll learn how smart communicators in Hollywood, on Madison Avenue, and even in our nation's capital make their messages simple and compelling to successfully capture people's attention—and how you can do the same.

IF ANY ONE INDUSTRY exemplifies our inability to pay attention, it's the movie industry. Folks who run Hollywood studios are well-known for having the attention span of a gnat and the memory of . . . well, we forget.

As a result, if you're going to make it in movies, you've got to make it fast. Savvy screenwriters know that to sell a film idea, they must boil it down to its absolute essence. This nugget is called "a high concept" or a "log line" (after how the screenplay is "logged" into a studio's production schedule), and it means being able to convey an idea in fewer than 25 words—if you can do it in 10 to 15, even better.

Since you probably never wanted to work in Hollywood, why are we recommending you adopt this movie-industry technique? Because it solves a huge communication problem: One of the major flaws we see in unsuccessful communication is that it's unfocused. By forcing you to reduce what you have to say to its very essence—the high concept—you can be fairly certain that your recipients will have a pretty good idea of what you are trying to say.

Odds are that in the past day or so, you:

- Got an e-mail message that was so all over the place that even a careful reading left you confused.

- Received a brochure that had so much detail that the main point got lost.
- Listened to a presentation that seemed to give a complete history of the topic, and somewhere in the middle you zoned out and now you can't remember what you heard about the history or anything else.

What's more, chances are that you committed exactly the same kind of error yourself. Often, the problem is that you're trying so hard to be comprehensive that you end up being ineffective. That's why we want you to go Hollywood (at least a little bit). Once you know how to develop a focused concept, you can use it as the basis for whatever message you want to convey, in any venue—from a cell-phone text message, to an e-mail, to a report, to an entire book.

Take this quick quiz to see how well you know movies based on their high concept descriptions (paraphrased from the official Academy Awards Web site, *www.oscar.com*).

1. The year is 1593, and budding playwright Will Shakespeare is suffering from writer's block until he falls in love with the beautiful Viola.

2. First-class passenger Rose is trapped in a loveless engagement when she meets steerage-class Jack on the maiden voyage of the *Titanic* luxury liner.

3. When the dying Roman emperor names the general Maximus as his heir, the emperor's jealous son betrays him and seizes the throne. Maximus soon becomes the fiercest fighter in Rome.

> Once you know how to develop a focused concept, you can use it as the basis for whatever message you want to convey, in any venue. ▶▶

4. In jazz age Chicago, two jailed murderesses compete with each other for newspaper headlines and the attention of their debonair attorney.

Did you find this quiz too easy? That means the high concepts for these films were successful. Each movie started with a strong idea, then the film's marketing supported the idea so that the audience (and the members of the Academy) was drawn in to want to experience it. Of course, that's not only a prescription for a hit film—and an Oscar—it's the formula for effective communication of any kind.

Quiz answers: 1. *Shakespeare in Love* (1998), 2. *Titanic* (1997), 3. *Gladiator* (2000), 4. *Chicago* (2002)

Coming soon to a theater near you?

A Web site called *scriptsales.com* **records every** movie deal: Once a studio agrees to put a screenplay (or concept) into production, a description pops up on the site. The majority of these movies never get made, but it's fun to see what Hollywood thinks is a viable movie idea. Here are the log lines (high concepts) of 3 projects, chosen at random, from June 2005:

● *Teacher of the Year.* Two junior high school instructors compete in a brutal battle to take teacher of the year honors.

● *Wedding Olympics.* The families of the bride and groom take on a competition of physical and mental games to determine which last name the couple will take.

● *The Untouchables: Capone Rising.* The story of the young Al Capone: his arrival in Chicago and his rise to criminal kingpin. Prequel to the 1987 film, *The Untouchables.*

There's no guarantee that these ideas will actually become films that play in your local multiplex (or even go straight to video). But there is no doubt what every finished film will be about. The descriptions are clear, crisp, and to the point. Therefore, they are the kind of messages you are trying to create, even if you don't write screenplays for a living.

"There's an old saying in Hollywood: If you can't describe your story in a sentence, there's something wrong with the story."

Rob Tobin, successful script doctor and author of How to Write High Structure, High Concept Movies

How it works

Let's start by understanding how the "high concept" or "log line"—works. As writer and director Peter Bohush (*Geezers*) writes, a log line is a "one-paragraph summary of a script that is often the sole basis for its consideration by Hollywood producers. But beneath the sales aspect of a log line, it is also used to determine if your story is, in fact, a solid screenplay worthy of becoming a movie." In other words, the necessity of clearly and succinctly stating the idea helps uncover whether the idea itself is sound.

High concept heads east

Hollywood screenwriters are not the only ones who understand the value of creating a high concept. The folks on the other coast—the smart marketers on Madison Avenue—have long known that the most persuasive message is a focused one.

Take Harry Beckwith, for instance. His book *Selling the Invisible*, published in 1997, was one of the bestselling business books of all time (so he must know something about creating a high concept and executing on it). Mr. Beckwith's key message: All "successful marketing starts with positioning."

Positioning "must be singular: One simple message," says Mr. Beckwith. "Your positioning must set you apart from your competitors. You must sacrifice. You cannot be all things to all people: You must focus on one thing."

To illustrate his point, Mr. Beckwith describes the "Grocery List Problem." If your mom sends you to the store to get milk, there's no problem: You go to the store, you get the milk, you bring it home.

◄◄ Successful marketing starts with positioning.

But if next time, Mom says, "Get raisins, Drano, Gummy Bears, milk, and some 100-watt light bulbs," you could very easily forget the milk. And maybe the milk was the thing Mom needed most, since the whole family is planning to have cereal for breakfast tomorrow.

"You run this risk," writes Mr. Beckwith, "when you hand prospects a grocery list of different messages about you. They remember the raisins, which aren't important, and forget the milk. Your prospects forget your real point of distinction and remember a supporting message that hardly matters."

The problem with taking the grocery list approach to communication is that the audience will find it hard to figure out what you are trying to say. ("Was the milk the important thing? Or the raisins?") And if it seems like too much work to your audience, they'll tune out and not retain any message about what you're trying to communicate.

Framing inside the Beltway

Last stop on our travels is Washington, D.C., where politicians know that, in order to keep doing whatever it is they do there, they have to be re-elected. As a result, they think a lot about how to create a compelling message that not only conveys their intention but also resonates with what really matters with voters. While Democrats and Republicans each have their own messages, they follow the same basic approach: The term of art both use is "framing."

A "frame" is a way of conveying an issue very simply and connecting it to the beliefs or values that the audience holds dear.

A "frame" is a way of conveying an issue very simply. ▶▶

Anything but elephants

George Lakoff, a professor of linguistics at the University of California at Berkeley, has long used a simple exercise in his courses to illustrate framing. He tells students, "Don't think of an elephant! Whatever you do, do not think of an elephant." Mr. Lakoff reports that he has never found a student who is able to do this. "Every word, like elephant, evokes a frame, which can be an image or other kinds of knowledge: Elephants are large, have floppy ears and a trunk, are associated with circuses, and so on. The word is defined relative to that frame. When we negate a frame, we evoke the frame."

According to George Lakoff, author of *Don't Think of an Elephant!* (2004) and the Democrats' expert on framing, "Frames are mental structures that shape the way we see the world. As a result, they shape the goals we seek, the plans we make, the way we act, and what counts as a good or bad outcome of our actions."

Frames are not tangible; they're conceptual. Mr. Lakoff explains that frames are part of what psychologists and scientists call "'the cognitive unconscious'—structures in our brains that we cannot consciously access, but know by their consequences: the way we reason and what counts as common sense." We know frames by language, he says, adding that "all words are defined relative to conceptual frames. When you hear a word, its frame (or collection of frames) is activated in your brain."

Framing is "not just language," Mr. Lakoff writes. "The ideas are primary—and the language carries those ideas, evokes those ideas."

President of framing

Although George Lakoff wrote the book on framing, the Democrats are actually playing catch-up in the battle to frame issues. Here is a sample of the frames that President George W. Bush has used to try to convince voters that his party's position is more desirable. Note that the frame positions the issue either more positively (attached to a value like faith) or negatively than the true meaning:

Frame	Meaning
Tax refund/relief	Tax cut
Opportunity scholarships	School vouchers for parents to send children to private schools
Faith-based programs.	Federal government charity to churches
Partial-birth abortion	Late-stage abortion
Exploring for energy	Drilling for oil

The best frames, especially in politics, are those that relate to people's inherent values. Values all Americans share include security, prosperity, opportunity, and freedom. To frame, Mr. Lakoff recommends choosing "the values most relevant to the frame you want to shift to. Try to win the argument at the values level."

Framing, 1, 2, 3

Now that you're back home after your whirlwind journey (Hollywood to New York to Washington, D.C.), how do you apply high concepts, positioning, and framing to your own communication? It's simple—so simple, in fact, that we can sum it up in the following 3 steps (*see following page*).

Again, notice that the message concept tells your audience what is in it for them—quickly. Don't expect your audience to extrapolate meanings, winnow it down, or even

---

3 steps to framing

1. Decide on the desired outcome of your communication.
   - "I want to inform our customers about our new return policy."
   - "I'd like to get funding approval for this project."
   - "I want customers to call us about this new addition to our product line."
2. Once you know the outcome you want, link it to the audience's need. Using the examples above, you could say:
   - "Customers told us our old return policy was confusing and felt unfair."
   - "This project will help my boss achieve an objective on his performance management plan (and help the company)."
   - "Our new product will cut the customer's energy costs."
3. Create a message concept—in 10 to 25 words—that meets the audience's need while achieving your objective.
   - "How our new return policy will make your life easier."
   - "Proposed project supports important objectives."
   - "Cut your energy costs by 14 percent just by using our product."

---

read it twice. Everyone in your audience has two questions: "What does this mean to me?" and "Why should I pay attention/care/take action?"

We've made this look easy, but we know it isn't. Most of us have grown so used to throwing everything and the kitchen sink in our communication that it hurts to hone it down to 1 single concept. But no one in your audience has the time or the patience to wade through a bunch of nonsense to get to the main point. They need to know immediately what your communication is about and will make an instantaneous decision about whether to read on or whether to tune out.

◄◄ No one in your audience has the time or the patience to wade through a bunch of nonsense.

Uncle Sam wants you

It's a winter's evening early in 2004, and you and your new girlfriend (3rd date) have decided to go to the movies together. In line to buy popcorn while you're waiting for the obscure Danish art film to start (you must really like her), you look around the lobby and notice the movie posters.

- There's a photo of Tom Cruise against a black background. He looks scary, and he's holding a large gun. The poster reads, "Collateral. It started like any other night."
- And there's a close-up of Leonardo DiCaprio with an intense look on his face. He's wearing large sunglasses that obscure his eyes; reflected in the lenses is a dramatic sky with big billowing clouds. "Imagine a life without limits," it says. "The Aviator."
- And over there is a hooded figure in red . . . oh, it's Spiderman holding a damsel in distress—of course, it's Kirsten Dunst—and they're high above New York City, with the Empire State Building in the background. The copy is spare: "Sacrifice. June 30."

During the Danish film (Really, really boring. Nothing happens. And it goes on at length. In Danish. With subtitles.),

What to do differently

✓ Say it quickly, simply, and so that your audience members know what's in it for them.

✓ Don't try to say too much or you may risk losing your audience's attention.

✓ Remember this phrase: "What is the one thing I need the audience to know or believe or do?"

66 You and I exist in an extraordinarily complicated stimulus environment, easily the most rapidly moving and complex that has ever existed on this planet. To deal with it, we need shortcuts. **99**

Robert B. Cialdini, author of Influence: The Psychology of Persuasion

you reflect on those movie posters. What makes them so compelling? And memorable? Then you realize: It's the simplicity, stupid. Designers of movie posters aren't trying to explain the plot; they're not trying to convey nuances or shading. Each movie poster is about one idea: one high concept.

The creators of these posters have only one thought in mind as they set out to create something to capture your attention. Everything falls away, except: "We need to get this concept across. And we need to do so on a wall in a crowded multiplex, as people are walking by on their way to a different movie."

Of course, posters are created to promote many other things besides movies. In fact, the poster has a long and storied history, because the idea of "posting" a notice or ad makes sense: People walk around towns and marketplaces, and they have to look at something, so why not advertise your play ("Shakespeare's latest"), your political candidate ("Vote for Taft"), or your product ("Coke. The pause that refreshes")?

In 1917, wanting to support the United States in its World War I efforts, the artist James Montgomery Flagg signed up to create patriotic posters. One of these works—a portrait of Uncle Sam pointing forcefully at the viewer with the words, "I Want You for U.S. Army"—would go on to become one of the most famous posters ever. Over 4 million copies were printed between 1917 and 1918, and the poster was later adapted to recruit troops during World War II as well.

The Uncle Sam poster works because it's direct, immediate, and arresting. It is communication reduced to a single image and a few compelling words. If you can boil your message down to this essential, you can communicate anything.

Even a Danish date movie.

5 | Fill in the blanks

In Chapter 4, you learned how to create a frame (a focus) for what you're trying to communicate. But how do you fill the frame to bring the concept to life? This chapter will help you paint a vivid and appealing picture (For your audience).

"WORDS! WORDS! WORDS! I'm so sick of words!" So sang the character of Eliza Doolittle in *My Fair Lady*, the Lerner and Loewe musical adaptation of the Pygmalion story, in which a rich professor transforms a poor girl into an upper class lady. Eliza was tired of how the men in her life constantly talked at her: her father, the professor who tried to change her, and now even Freddy, the man who professed to adore her. As she sang to Freddy, she'd had it:

> *"Don't talk of stars burning above;*
> *If you're in love, show me!*

We understand her frustration. The information overload that we described in Chapter 1 has created another challenge for those of us attempting to communicate: It has made talk—and the use of words—cheap. (As Eliza sings: "Say one more word and I'll scream!")

In a world where it's so easy to create and convey volumes of content, words lose their uniqueness and become an undistinguished meaningless mass.

To illustrate, here's a metaphor. It's a cold December day in the Berkshire Mountains of western Massachusetts, and the breeze carries the subtle but unmistakable scent of snow. You stand in the stillness for a moment, and suddenly you feel something whisper across your cheek. You lift your head to the sky to experience the beginning of the season's first snowfall. Catching a flake on your mitten, you look at the lacy pattern and wonder: Is it true that no two are alike?

But in a few minutes, the storm has turned into a full-fledged snow squall. With precipitation at the rate of an inch or 2 an hour, the road is soon covered with snow, the landscape obscured by white. A few hours later, you're no longer exulting at the beauty of the storm—instead, you're wondering if you'll be able to get back to Boston in this blizzard. You get the metaphor:

> *Words are like snow. One is extraordinary, a moderate quantity is beautiful, but too much is simply a big white mess.*

And by the time March rolls around, after 85 inches of the stuff, the novelty has completely worn off—you want nothing more than for the snow to stop already.

As someone who wants to get people's attention, how do you deal with the fact that words have become a commodity? We have already talked about the importance of keeping your message focused. To that we now add: You need to make it (extremely) tangible as well. To be blunt: Vague and conceptual don't cut it. And you can't count on your audience to connect the dots, because they won't.

To explain what we mean, we turn first to Christopher Locke, author of *Cluetrain Manifesto, Gonzo Marketing,* and *The Bombast Transcripts.* If you want a mind-expanding experience, Mr. Locke's your man—his ideas make you think. And one of the things he makes you think about is how counterproductive it is to be vague.

Vague and conceptual don't cut it. ▶▶

In *Gonzo Marketing*, Mr. Locke takes on the challenge of achieving or even defining a term used all the time in marketing: "the value proposition."

Mr. Locke writes that "business in general and marketing in particular seem to assume we know what they mean when they sling around terms like value, brand, and positioning and equate the resulting blur of vague ideas to something we might actually care about."

The reality is most people don't know what these things mean; and if you ask 10 people who think they do to define the concepts, you get 10 different explanations.

Sense and sensibility

Even if you've never read a Jane Austen novel, you've probably seen a film version (guys: just think "date movie"). *Pride and Prejudice, Mansfield Park, Emma,* and the others all depict a long-ago era before the modern age. A time without electricity, or phones, or Starbucks with WiFi. Mass entertainment consisted of books and other publications, and letters via post were the only way to communicate with someone who was far away.

You had to take out a piece of paper, write by hand using a quill pen, put the paper in an envelope, mail it, and wait a week, a month, or longer for a response.

As a result, words were precious. They were chosen carefully. With no delete key, no "track and accept changes," no "cut and paste," you had to think carefully about what you wanted to say before you put pen to paper.

And when the words were received, they were treated with deference—pored over, read aloud, reread to savor their meaning.

Those were the days.

"Jargon is the verbal sleight of hand that makes the old hat seem newly fashionable; it gives an air of novelty . . . to ideas that, if stated directly, would seem superficial, stale, frivolous, or false.**"**

David Lehman, critic and editor of **American Poetry**

The problem isn't limited to marketing terms. What does any buzzword—quality, innovation, cost-efficiency, progress, or customer service—really represent? They're all a bunch of jargon and, as such, abstractions that you can't connect to. Most are long words, so they seem important, but you can't touch, taste, see, smell, or hear any of these concepts. My sense of what "quality" looks like may be cool and blue, while yours may be square, stark, and white.

Thick description

What's needed to cut through all this abstraction, says Christopher Locke, is something called "thick description." That was the term used in the 1970s by anthropologist Clifford Geertz to address a challenge he had when trying to write about the societies he studied.

When Mr. Geertz tried to step back and give a big-picture view of what he observed, two things happened:

First, because the description was so conceptual, it wasn't very compelling—you just weren't that interested in the society in question, because you couldn't picture it.

And second, those general descriptions also carried the bias of the anthropologist, because concepts (and jargon) are often judgmental. ("Quality" must be a good thing, right?)

To address the problem, Mr. Geertz discovered that the more specific he was, the better he was able to bring the people of Java or Morocco to life—and the problems of bias fell away. Everything got more real, more immediate, more true.

To illustrate, Mr. Geertz, in his book _The Interpretation of Culture,_ tells a story of a Jewish shopkeeper who is robbed by a sheikh's goon squad in colonial North Africa in 1916. Because the French troops in charge won't act on the matter ("Mon Dieu! We don't want to get involved!"), the shopkeeper hires some local muscle of his own to steal the sheikh's sheep as payment for his loss.

When the shopkeeper is discovered as being the person behind the robbery, the sheikh doesn't kill him; he listens to the shopkeeper's claim that prompted hiring the muscle and agrees that it's only fair for the shopkeeper to take 500 sheep in payment.

The story gives a "thicker" and more accurate description of what culture was like in colonial North Africa—how terms like justice and retribution played out—than simply using the terms themselves.

"Small facts speak to large issues," writes Mr. Geertz, "because they were meant to."

As Christopher Locke explains, "thick description, while it may seem confusing, often comes closer to what's actually going on than would 'thin description'—the kind of

Diamonds in the details

The Canadian novelist Carol Shields (1935–2003) was a master of bringing characters to life by using details. Her 10 novels (one of which, *The Stone Diaries,* won the Pulitzer Prize for fiction), 3 collections of stories, and 3 volumes of poetry all used descriptions of domesticity to help readers vividly imagine the world Ms. Shields had created.

As she wrote in 1998, "I wanted wallpaper in my novels, cereal bowls, cupboards, cousins, buses, local elections, head colds, cramps, newspapers, and I abandoned Chekhov's dictum that if there is a rifle hanging over the fireplace, it must go off before the story ends. A rifle could hang over a fireplace for countless other reasons. For atmosphere, to give texture, to comment on the owner of the house, to ignite a scene with its presence, not its ammunition."

35,000 feet

It's a consistent flight path. Airplanes arriving from California, Chicago, and other points west always follow the same route when flying into the Newark airport: They sweep in from the north, through New York State's Orange County, then down through northern New Jersey to runway 22R or 22L

That means the planes fly directly over Alison's New Jersey town. You can see them high overhead, already well into their descent as they turn to the south to make their approach.

But, from the window seat of the plane, even when you pay close attention, it's difficult to identify anything specific on the ground. Alison knows the area very well—has lived here nearly her entire life—and can tell you where nearly anything is. (Especially if it involves retail: "Out on Route 17, the Crate & Barrel is south of the Home Depot, which is across the highway from Home Goods, which. . . .")

But it all looks so different from the plane. There is no telling detail. One flat roof—of a warehouse or a big box store—looks like every other flat roof. Whole neighborhoods are obscured by trees. Roads are interchangeable when all you can see is dark asphalt and the bright yellow line down the middle.

The pilot says, "We've begun our initial descent . . ." and you stare down hopefully, but the world you know really isn't recognizable at 35,000, 25,000, even 10,000 feet above the earth. We're so dependent on the details that a bird's eye (plane's eye?) view is too conceptual for us to really get our bearings, no matter how well we know the terrain.

Vague, conceptional, or jargon-laden communication is just like that. We know there is a message in there somewhere, just like we know that there is a very nice suburb filled with secluded ponds and countless soccer fields down below, but we can't see it.

We'll make an effort for a few minutes. Then our eyes glaze over and we just stop trying.

succinct clear-cut abstraction that appears perfectly plausible, but totally distorts reality."

He's right. Which is more effective, the story about the shopkeeper and the sheep, or a long sentence stating that "justice in North Africa was capricious"? Abstractions don't draw people in—they create a screen that makes your audience tune out because there is nothing compelling to capture attention. Big words like "capricious" are vague and off-putting. Why would anyone (except a graduate student) want to pay attention?

Create communication that your audience can see, hear, smell, taste, and touch. ▶▶

Let's get specific

The concept of thick description sounds intriguing, but how do you apply it to your work? Start by engaging the senses: Create communication that your audience can see, hear, smell, taste, and touch.

Do you dream in color? Or remember your dreams at all? Whether or not your dreams are memorable enough to analyze with your therapist, the truth is that we all have a multiplex in our heads, ready to play movies 24/7—when we're asleep, for sure, or even when we're fully conscious.

Think of your favorite film. (For Paul, it's the 1988 movie *Die Hard* starring Bruce Willis.) Now close your eyes and try to picture a scene from that beloved movie. Isn't it just like playing a DVD? Can't you recall almost everything perfectly: The setting? The characters' expressions? The dialogue (or, in the case of *Die Hard*, lack of dialogue)? What happens first, and next, and after that?

This ability to play scenes in your brain works not only for actual movies, but for firsthand memories as well. Remember your first kiss? Or, if you are a Red Sox fan, the last pitch of game 4 of the 2004 World Series, when the Sox won their first championship since 1918? Or the time you tried sky diving?

And your brain's amazing "I can picture it" imagination applies to not just sight and hearing, but to all 5 senses. You can, in an instant, vividly recall the scent of lemons being squeezed or popcorn popping, the taste of pepperoni pizza or bubblegum, the sensation of your finger rubbing across sandpaper or an ice cube on your hot neck.

The point is that human beings may have an evolved brain, but we're wired to our senses, irresistibly drawn

Hit 'em where it hurts

In *Die Hard,* Bruce Willis plays John McClane, a New York street cop who has traveled to Los Angeles on Christmas Eve to meet (and hopefully reconcile with) his estranged wife (Bonnie Bedelia) at her company Christmas party, which takes place in a high-rise office tower.

When he gets there, John decides to try out a tip he heard about combating jet lag: He takes off his shoes and makes "fists" with his toes. Unfortunately, in the middle of this exercise, he is interrupted by a gang of German terrorists who are trying to steal gold worth hundreds of millions of dollars. John McClane must defeat the terrorists and free the hostages—and he must do so barefoot, without any weapons or help.

In Paul's favorite scene, the terrorists are chasing John, trying to kill him, and they have cornered him in a computer room with glass walls. They shoot many rounds of ammunition, shattering glass and sending it everywhere. The only way for John to escape is to walk across broken glass.

While film critics may disagree with Paul as to what represents artistically significant cinema, they can't deny that the previous scene hits audiences in the gut and sole—if not the gut and soul. (OUCH!)

Infomercial-o-matic

If anyone understands how being specific can attract an audience (and, more importantly, sell products) it's the folks who produce infomercials. And the royal family of the "spiel"—selling innovative products that you just have to buy—are the Popeils, who began selling their wares in the 1930s and have brought the world such classics as:

- The Veg-O-Matic: "Slices, wedges, dices whole foods in one stroke!"
- Mr. Microphone: "Put your voice on FM radio!"
- The Showtime Rotisserie: "Cut the fat . . . naturally!"

The scion of this dynasty is Ron Popeil, who built on his father's huckster legacy by founding a company called Ronco, which has generated more than $2 billion in sales in 4 decades. Ron Popeil (famous for his phrase, "But wait! There's more!") invented the infomercial whose centerpiece is the demonstration: Yes, the person pitching talks (and talks and talks) about the product, but just as important is showing every detail about what the product does. Here's an excerpt from a 1956 infomercial for a product called Chop-O-Matic (from *But Wait! There's More!* by Timothy Samuelson):

"For chopping celery, place your celery under the container—a few taps—your chopping chores are over and your celery is finely chopped." (Celery is shown before chopping and after.)

"For those delicious potato pancakes, place your potatoes under the machine—a few taps—a few seconds—those potato pancakes won't fall apart, and they won't be tasteless and rubbery as when you grate them." (The host starts with a big pile of potatoes and ends up with sizzling potato pancakes. Boy, do they look good.)

"I'll show the crowning feature of this marvelous new machine, for now, you can chop three or four whole onions at one time. Here's where your Chop-O-Matic will save the day for both your hands and your eyes. You chop those onions so fine, all your onions are chopped to perfection without shedding a single tear." (Onions, onions, and more onions. And a smiling tear-free cook.)

"But wait! There's more! As a special bonus, you will receive at no additional charge, a valuable recipe book containing fifty secret recipes by world-famous chefs."

Who could resist? Let's order before midnight so we don't forget.

to what we can see, hear, smell, taste, or touch. And you can use this phenomenon to your advantage when communicating, to draw your audience in and get them to pay attention.

Here's an example. When *Fortune* magazine was founded in 1930, its publisher Henry Robinson Luce wrote that the new publication's mission was to "accurately, vividly, and concretely" describe modern business—in other words, to bring business to life so you can touch it, feel it, experience it. And in a 1935 article about newspaper magnate William Randolph Hearst, the story's writer delivered on that mission. Rather than simply citing facts about the extent of Hearst Corporation's lines of business, revenues, and profits, the article made Mr. Hearst tangible:

> *Picture a room in California. In the middle of the big room, in a big chair, sits a big man. He has a long face like a horse, a thick neck, big clumsy bones, and when he turns to look at you his ice-cold blue eyes bore into your soul. On the priceless carpet at his feet there are spread six newspapers worth altogether from twelve to eighteen cents. . . . The old man—he is seventy-two—is hanging over them with a big black pencil in his hand. Every so often he reaches down and makes a cryptic black mark.*

The details are vivid enough that nearly 75 years later, you are transported to that room in California, where the big man marked up his newspapers. And you are intrigued enough to stay with the story to learn more.

Make specific details work for you

But you're thinking: I don't write profiles of William Randolph Hearst or sell Veg-O-Matics—I'm just a humble manager trying to communicate humble (sometimes boring) topics. How do I use description to appeal to my audience?

Determine ways you can be less conceptual and more specific. ▶▶

Start by looking at your current communication and determining ways you can make it less conceptual and more specific. For instance, Alison's company has an electronic newsletter called *Smart Tips* that it sends out to clients and prospects every 2 weeks. The newsletter features "news you can use"—suggestions and advice that customers can put to work to improve their communication practices.

A recent issue of *Smart Tips* (*www.davisandco.com .resources/samples/smarttips.html*) was designed to address the challenge of communicating human resource (HR) issues to employees. Here was the first draft of the lead paragraph:

USING HR COMMUNICATION VEHICLES FOR WHAT THEY DO BEST

How can human resource professionals and the communicators who support them ensure they're satisfying employees' HR information needs? The first step is to treat employees as consumers of your communication and determine how to effectively reach and engage each segment of your work force. The more you know about what appeals to your audience, the more successful you'll be at using HR communication vehicles for what they do best.

Not terrible, but a little thin—too conceptual and abstract, and teetering on the edge of jargon. But what if the focus was sharpened a bit and we added a more vivid, specific description of what happens when HR communication doesn't work? Here's the second draft (see following page).

USING HR COMMUNICATION VEHICLES FOR WHAT THEY DO BEST

How can human resources professionals ensure that employees will open and access the communication you provide to them? In today's information-overloaded world, even important HR material may get lost in the shuffle: buried in a blizzard of e-mail, misplaced in a crowded intranet, and tossed aside with the day's junk mail. The first step to solving this problem is to truly understand your employees' communication preferences. Here's how.

The idea was to get the audience to picture "getting lost in the shuffle": "a blizzard of e-mail . . . and tossed aside with the day's junk mail." Can't you just see it?

⮕ INSIGHT 5:
Wretched excess

Caution: You can be too descriptive. And you can try too hard to tell a story. In fact, although a little flavor is a good thing, too much can cause a really bad case of indigestion.

For instance, let Edward George Bulwer-Lytton be a lesson to you. In 1830, Mr. Lytton was then a young writer who decided to create a novel called *Paul Clifford*. He probably wanted to grab the reader by the lapels (or whatever they wore in those days) and forcibly yank him into the story; otherwise, how could you explain this first sentence?

It was a dark and stormy night; the rain fell in torrents—except in occasional intervals, when it was checked by a violent gust of wind which swept up the streets (for it is in London that our scene lies), rattling along the housetops, and fiercely agitating the scanty flame of the lamps that struggled against the darkness.

Chewy, isn't it? Although you might be tempted to make allowances for the fact that writing was more flowery in the 19th century, Mr. Lytton was actually taken to task by contemporary critics for having a writing style that was "archaic": lots of juicy adjectives. In any case, something about that first phrase struck a chord, and "it was a dark and stormy night" came to personify writing—and later, movies—that were unabashedly over the top. And in the mid-20th century, "a dark and stormy night" reached its zenith when cartoonist Charles Schultz (in a little comic strip you may have heard of named *Peanuts*) needed to give his character Snoopy a new occupation. It was time for the beagle to become a novelist. Snoopy wasn't a very good writer, but he had a certain canine panache:

> *It was a dark and stormy night. Suddenly, a shot rang out! A door slammed. The maid screamed.*
> *Suddenly, a pirate ship appeared on the horizon!*
> *While millions of people were starving, the king lived in luxury. Meanwhile, on a small farm in Kansas, a boy was growing up.*

What to do differently

✓ Avoid abstractions and vague concepts.

✓ Appeal to the senses by using specific descriptions to help your audience connect by seeing, hearing, smelling, tasting, and touching.

✓ Don't be afraid to make your communication just a little longer (if you absolutely must) to make it more tangible.

"Thick description" captures layered, rich, and contextual meaning by being concrete and specific. As a result, it brings your message to life.

Fast-forward to the early 1980s, when a graduate student named Scott Rice was assigned to write a paper about a minor Victorian novelist and chose Mr. Lytton. A couple of years later, as a professor of English at San Jose State University, Mr. Rice decided to pay tribute to Mr. Lytton—and all the writers who just can't stop the flow of adjectives—by creating an annual contest for hyperbolic first paragraphs.

The response has been overwhelming. Thousands of would-be Lyttons (or Snoopys) have entered their attempts at excessive description. Take, for example, the winning entry for 2000, penned by Sera Kirk, from Vancouver, BC:

> *A small assortment of astonishingly loud brass instruments raced each other lustily to the respective ends of their distinct musical choices as the gates flew open to release a torrent of tawny fur comprised of angry yapping bullets that nipped at Desdemona's ankles, causing her to reflect once again (as blood filled her sneakers and she fought her way through the panicking crowd) that the annual Running of the Pomeranians in Liechtenstein was a stupid idea.*

Isn't that great? But unless you want to win the Bulwer-Lytton Fiction Contest, we have advice, which can be summed up in just a few words: Please don't try this at home (or in the office, for that matter).

6 | Tell a story

By now, you've probably noticed that we tell a lot of stories. We don't just give general advice, we share an account of something that happened, will happen, or could happen, involving a character you can relate to. Telling stories is an effective way to attract people's interest—and keep them interested. As you go about trying to grab the attention of your audience, it is a technique we think you should use often. This chapter is devoted to discussing how.

TODAY, WE MAY FEEL pretty darn modern, buying our organic groceries at Whole Foods, driving home in our hybrid Toyota Prius, and cooking dinner on our Viking range—but human beings are still wired the way we were in prehistoric times, when we hunted and gathered our food out in the wild, walked home barefoot, and burned mastodon meat on the campfire.

After dinner, we still want to spend our time the same way today as we did back then: listening to stories. Of course, in the cave we told our own stories and listeners had to imagine the video portion. Today, we watch *Desperate Housewives* on the flat-screen TV, but it's essentially the same script: hunky guys, sexy women, mystery, intrigue, sometimes mayhem.

"Storytelling" has gotten a bad rep recently: It's become a management fad, the subject of way too many business books, an "art form" that seems to require a mystical approach, complete with a dowsing rod and scented oils.

That's not what we're talking about. We're talking about taking what you do all the time—telling a story about what happened over the weekend or on your vacation—and applying this technique to the communication you do at work.

The origin of stories

Why did our ancestors tell stories? According to Reading Is Fundamental, the nation's oldest and largest nonprofit children's literacy organization, there are several reasons why storytelling is an integral part of just about every culture. Researchers believe that storytelling was used to:

- Teach history
- Make sense of the world
- Satisfy a need for entertainment
- Explain supernatural forces
- Communicate experiences to others
- Record what happened for the benefit of future generations and for posterity
- Help children learn language.

Stories are effective not only as a form of entertainment but also as a way to communicate any topic. Since humans are hard-wired to stop when the story starts, a story instantly captures our attention—whether it's a tale of two cities or a simple little anecdote about how you made the irate customer happy, despite the odds.

Here's why stories are so powerful:

- *We want to be entertained, not lectured to.* A story makes us think, "This is going to be fun," not "Am I going to be tested on this?"
- *Stories teach subtly and indirectly.* Instead of hitting us over the head, stories imply the message. As historian

and social philosopher Hannah Arendt said, "Storytelling reveals meaning without committing the error of defining it."

- *Stories allow emotion to be expressed*—and that's secretly appealing. In most other forms of "official" communication, emotion is off-limits. Yet we (even men) are actually drawn to emotions: We want to laugh, cry, be scared, and feel better afterward. That is a heck of a lot better than another boring memo or a 10-page corporate white paper.

- *Stories feel genuine, not packaged or spun.* As Christopher Locke writes in *Gonzo Marketing*, the Internet has created a new "campfire" that encourages the free exchange of stories. "We have gotten used to talking amongst ourselves in uncontrived, unpremeditated human voices," and now companies have to do the same. "Not the smarmy, cloyingly sentimental 'human interest' stories businesses are so fond of leveraging in support of some arcane brand mysticism, but rather, stories that come from actually grappling with the . . . problem the service purports to solve."

- *The experience of a story draws people together.* Here's Christopher Locke again (who is obviously a strong advocate of the power of stories): "The best stories can become myths that draw people together, create entire cultures. The people within the culture so created are not strangers to each other precisely because they know the old stories. They share and reflect on them. They remember together. This creates powerful cohesion, even identity."

◀◀ We want to laugh, cry, be scared, and feel better afterward.

Even the *Harvard Business Review* (HBR)—not a publication anyone would accuse of being lighthearted, frivolous, or even remotely New Age—uses storytelling to engage readers and convey information. The centerpiece of HBR's use of story is a regular feature called "The HBR Case Study," which presents a fictionalized account of a business challenge, and then asks real-life experts to provide advice on how to solve the challenge. Here's the first paragraph of the case study from the April 2005 issue:

> *Jim Hargrove's startled expression would have been amusing had he not been in such a pitiable state. He was standing in the yacht's magnificently appointed galley, wondering if his stomach would be able to hold down the cola he was pouring into a crystal flute, when his colleague, Rita Sanchez, said something outrageous. Now the drink had spilled down the length of his pleated khakis, and he was sputtering, "You aren't seriously suggesting that we reduce prices by 50 percent. Are you?"*

HBR doesn't restrict the use of story to these case studies—storytelling, especially those involving real people, appears in many of the articles in the publication. The reason is simple: because it creates a more compelling "door" to the article, drawing readers in and bringing abstract concepts to life.

Here's another example, this one from September 2005:

> *A few years ago, a middle manager . . . came to see me upon his promotion to a senior*

management role. I'll call him Tobin Holmes. . . .
A young Englishman who had studied classics
at Oxford before graduating in the top 5% of
his class at Insead [the French business school],
Holmes was very clever. But he feared he couldn't
take on the new job's responsibilities. At the root
of Holmes's dilemma was his suspicion that he
was just not good enough, and he lived in dread
that he would be exposed at any moment.

The reader becomes engaged and interested in the rest of the article in a way they weren't before. Why? Because they can see, and, most importantly, *feel* themselves or someone they know in it. (Who hasn't had—at some point in their career—a boss or responsibility that they felt overwhelmed by?) Now the article isn't about some new management theory or some overpriced management consultant's recollection—it's about them. Remember the advice in Chapter 2—any communication, even stories, should always ask, "Et tu?"

How to tell a story

We don't think we really need to teach you how to tell a story; you know already, because you tell stories all the time—to friends, family, coworkers.

But we've discovered that many of us who can tell great stories at a family barbecue freeze up when it's time to use stories to communicate something professional or important. It's as if we took off the comfortable T-shirt and shorts and put on a formal, uncomfortable suit—we stiffen up and get stuffy.

So, to help you get looser, here are 6 things to keep in mind when telling your story:

1. Keep your focus on the audience

As we described in Chapter 2, you need to keep the audience's needs and preferences firmly at the forefront. What is it about your story that will be meaningful to them? After all, the reason you are telling the story is to get something across.

2. Have a single message or moral

This relates to Chapter 4 on creating a high concept. We all have had the experience of being at a party and finding ourselves trapped by someone who has launched into a long story about . . . well, it's impossible to tell, really.

At a party, this is annoying but not devastating. You smile politely, slowly move away, and get yourself another cheese puff. However, if you are trying to communicate something to an audience, this kind of (pointless) storytelling is fatal. You need to make sure you get your concept across.

3. Structure your story with a beginning, middle, and end

You want the story to flow. One way to do it is to divide your story into 3 parts:

- In part 1 you introduce the characters and the obstacles they face.
- Part 2 is devoted to how the characters deal with the problem.
- And part 3 describes the resolution.

Google vs. Grandmom

David Berkowitz, who writes a column for the online newsletter *Search Insider*, used the character of his grandmother to tell a story about how confusing the online search function is.

"I'm so stupid," she said, either to the computer or to me, or perhaps both.

My poor grandmother. She survived the Nazis, the Russians, and the Poles. She braved postwar anti-Semitism in Germany. She immigrated to the United States with her husband (my namesake) and two children, raising them on a chicken farm in New Jersey. This woman has known hardships the likes of which I could never imagine.

Now, with my help, she's trying to fulfill her greatest challenge: mastering the Internet.

Even knowing her life resume, I'm convinced this is one challenge she can't win. But it's not her fault. The Internet's simply too powerful to be simple. A computer is not just a TV upgrade, just as newspapers were not just an upgrade from the town crier. As easy as the point, click, search concept may be for us, the Web's on-ramp is slanted a little too deep to accommodate everyone.

I've also realized that for my grandmother, searching in general is counterintuitive. She always has an answer to everything. I could just picture her response if someone suggested that she turn to a search engine for answers.

On searching for driving directions: "You think I don't know where I'm going?"

On searching for product recommendations, "And I should trust some [insert choice Yiddish word here] instead of calling Mrs. Reisman who's been living next door in the same house over 35 years and [insert choice non-sequitur: still goes for a walk every morning/always serves my favorite grapes when we play cards/donates every month one hundred dollars to charity]?"

It's not just a story about the Internet anymore—it's got drama and humor.

Fairy tales are great examples of classically structured stories. They begin, "Once upon a time," and introduce you to the person who the story is going to be about. (A poor but sweet girl.) Then they introduce the conflict. (A wicked stepmother and a bunch of even more rotten stepsisters. A prince looking for true love. A fancy ball. A glass slipper.) Finally, fairy tales describe how the problem was overcome. (In the whole kingdom, the glass slipper only fit her foot) and move to the resolution. (They lived happily ever after.)

Of course, this is not the only possible story structure. Many stories are reversed—for example, the sappy best-selling 1970 novel *Love Story* (by Erich Segal) starts with the (not happily-ever-after) resolution: "What can you say about a twenty-five year-old girl who died?" You can use any structure you want. Just make sure it supports the message you want to get across.

4. Create characters
You don't need Superman or Winston Churchill to be the hero of your story: The main character can be you (as funny and flawed as you are), or even better, your audience. But whenever possible you want to give the audience someone to identify with or root for. (Think Cinderella.)

5. Include the facts
Every newspaper reporter answers 5 essential questions every time he or she writes a story: who, what, where, when, and why. Even if it's as basic as a 50-word article announcing the opening of a new shipping facility, you need to make sure all 5 questions have been answered.

Here's an example we made up to demonstrate how to tell a story while including all essential information. We have flagged the who, what, where, when, and why:

It took three years, two different architects, and the facilities team working three shifts seven days a week for three months, but the new satellite shipping warehouse [THE WHAT] opened on schedule in Des Moines [WHERE] on Saturday [WHEN].

"Being able to ship from the middle of the country will allow us to get our products to our customers faster," [WHY] said Patrick Pass, senior vice president of logistics [WHO] at Acme Widgets. "This facility will give us an advantage over our competitors who only have shipping centers on the East or West Coast."

6. Develop dramatic tension

What is going to occur? How will it end? Will it all turn out okay? What makes a story a story is action—something has to happen. That means that whether you are developing a long story or one you could tell in an elevator ride, the story must have a plot.

Unless you're creating a love story, odds are that "boy meets girl; boy loses girl; boy gets girl back" (with or without singing and dancing) is not going to work as the plot for your story.

But there's one universal plot that works every time, we think because it's the basis for every story: overcoming obstacles. From Romeo and Juliet to Spiderman to the guy in the next cubicle talking about the time his school played Notre Dame—(where his hopelessly outmatched alma mater used every bit of ingenuity and grit they had . . . and only lost by 14)—every story is about the struggle to overcome something: disapproving parents, the Evil Villain, or eating too many hamburgers and drinking too much beer at the tailgating party.

7 (or more?) plots

Storytelling experts maintain that there are a finite number of variations of a plot—the number most often cited is 7. But the experts don't agree about what the 7 plots are.

Here's one list:

1. Rags to riches
2. The quest (including overcoming insurmountable obstacles)
3. Voyage and return
4. The hero as monster (or monster as hero)
5. Rebirth
6. Fish out of water
7. Boys meets girl

Here's another variation:

1. Man (or woman) versus nature
2. Man versus man
3. Man versus the environment
4. Man versus machines/technology
5. Man versus supernatural/aliens
6. Man versus self
7. Man versus god/religion

Others think that seven plots is too limiting, so they come with their own more expansive lists. Ronald B. Tobias, author of *20 Master Plots*, looks at plot variations this way:

Quest	*Metamorphosis*
Adventure	*Transformation*
Pursuit	*Maturation*
Rescue	*Love*
Escape	*Forbidden love*
Revenge	*Sacrifice*
The riddle	*Discovery*
Rivalry	*Wretched excess*
Underdog	*Ascension*
Temptation	*Descension*

Putting stories into practice

These guidelines discussed here are just suggestions; you need to tell your story your way, in a way that resonates with your audience. As you've read in this book, we use stories a lot, in many circumstances, and, quite frankly, we often break our own rules if we think doing so will make the story stronger.

The sidebar on the following page is a story Alison used in her weblog (*www.davisandco.com/blog*) to illustrate what happens when a senior executive reacts badly to feedback.

The trouble with feedback: A true story

The division president was very angry.
He was angry that the communication manager at a facility where a segment of his employees worked (along with those of other divisions) had included his employees in a communication assessment without consulting him. He was angry that his employees in the assessment study were "negative" about his quarterly all-hands meetings. Employees thought those sessions could be a lot more effective.

And he was angry at me because my firm conducted the assessment and wrote the report. I had been summoned to a meeting with the division president and his staff to explain (i.e., defend) our findings. The intention was to browbeat me into "admitting" that the feedback wasn't true. Only trouble was, it was true: we reported exactly what those employees said. They liked the notion of the all-hands meetings, but they knew the meetings could be more meaningful, and they had helpful suggestions.

It was a shame that the division president was too angry to listen. In fact, he was ready to cancel future all-hands events. He had invested a lot of time and energy into those sessions, he said, and if employees didn't appreciate them, why should he continue?

At our meeting, I didn't say much. The division president was demonstrating very clearly that he wouldn't listen to anything that could be construed as negative. "Constructive criticism" did not appear to be a term the president was familiar with. And I was very aware that my firm was in danger of being fired.

As the president glowered, I thought about the trouble with feedback. It's risky. You have to be open to the notion that people will have viewpoints that may be critical, messy, irrational, demanding, unappreciative, and, very possibly, quite brilliant. This honesty may make you uncomfortable. It may make you mad.

What happens next is key. Do you get over yourself (and your ego), settle down, and listen to what these folks have to say? Or, like the division president, do you shut down, become spiteful, and punish the people who honestly shared their perspectives?

Spite and small-mindedness won the day for the division president. I heard later that he stopped bringing his town-hall meetings to that facility; employees could call in, if they wanted, but he was damned if he would actually travel to see that ungrateful group face-to-face.

Guess he showed them.

“ Listen to Steve Jobs talk about the latest offering from Pixar, the creators of the Myst video game series and epics like the Flaming Lips' *Yoshimi Battles the Pink Robots* and Jay Z's *Black Album*. Their creators all say that, no matter how flashy the effects, in the end it's all about story: A compelling narrative, an original voice, and characters both relatable and wondrous. **”**

Kevin Smokler, editor of Bookmark Now

Elevating the mundane through stories

We even use stories to bring life to the most workaday communication. The following "message platform" that Alison first created for a client company we'll call "Visal," is hardly *Die Hard*, but it does use several of the storytelling guidelines: character (in this example, it's the company), dramatic tension, and essential facts:

> *Our competition is tougher than ever. Our customers increasingly demand more, but they want to pay less. And the internal processes that worked well five years ago (or even last year) simply can't keep pace with what we need to do to be competitive.*
>
> *That's why Visal needs to change, and change quickly. We simply won't survive, much less achieve our vision, unless we do things differently.*
>
> *Like many leading companies, we are beginning our efforts in areas that will make the most impact—in our case, on operations. Our new change program is designed to make dramatic improvements to three core operational areas: customer-directed activities, purchasing processes, and financial operations.*
>
> *The idea, quite simply, is to be smarter and more efficient. We need to be leaner. Less bureaucratic. More transparent. And more systematic.*
>
> *These changes will be broad and deep and will have a significant impact on employees, especially those who work in these areas. People will have to learn new skills. Their jobs will change. They'll have to do things differently. And in some cases, employees will be reassigned or even let go.*

It would be great if we could make these changes without affecting employees. But that's not realistic. Visal has been very successful. And we have tremendous confidence that we will be a leader in the future. But in an increasingly competitive business environment, we can't stand still. We've got to take risks, make significant improvements, and act now.

Keep it short

One of the biggest pitfalls in telling stories is being like the Energizer Bunny: You keep on going and going and going . . .

Cavemen didn't have this problem. Maybe it was because life expectancies were shorter. Or there were no batteries. Or it took so darn long to carve those drawings onto the walls that they didn't want to add more detail than absolutely necessary.

Whatever the reason, cavemen kept their stories short, as this recent "translation" of a pictograph from a cave in Borneo shows:

Cronk went out looking for his future mate on a Saturday night, only to return alone. As he walked in with a black eye and missing a couple of teeth, he explained to his cave-mate what happened.

"Me hit her over the head, and started to drag her back, but she woke up, hit me, and went home to her mother. Cronk alone as always."

In just 28 words, Cronk explained why he was spending another Saturday night alone. Cavemen were brief. You should be, too. (For more on how to keep it short, see Chapter 9.) How do you know if you have been going on for too long? If you feel compelled to use the phrase, "to make a long story short," get out your scissors.

INSIGHT 6:
Hemingway c'est moi

We never aspired to write literature—never wanted to spend our days starving in a freezing garret (starving, freezing: bad), producing a finely crafted tender coming-of-age novel about a young man accepting his cosmic destiny as a water-park manager in the Wisconsin Dells.

But we did like the idea of making a comfortable living (comfortable: good) communicating. Telling compelling stories to get people's attention and make a difference (and getting paid for it)—that had definite appeal.

But, as Paul learned early in his career, although telling stories sounds like a sweet deal (money for nothing?), it's not as easy as it looks.

Paul was 25 years old and working as a feature writer for the New Jersey newspaper *The Star-Ledger*, when he was hired by *Forbes* magazine. He was the youngest reporter in the history of the business magazine. The man who hired Paul, then editor-in-chief James Walker Michaels,

What to do differently

✓ Use real (if necessary, disguised) or even fictional characters to jump-start your communication and draw in the audience.

✓ Remember that your story needs to have a plot—something has to happen, or be poised to happen, otherwise your story is not a story.

✓ Be aware of all the examples of story around you, and analyze what makes them so compelling: from the middle column of the *Wall Street Journal*'s front page, to video games, to advertising, there are great stories going on everywhere.

was legendary. The man invented what we now think of when we think of business journalism.

Michaels (as he was referred to by all) was also famous for his temper—he didn't suffer fools gladly; heck, he didn't suffer most people at all, and his bellowing in the halls in the *Forbes* New York City offices was commonplace.

But perhaps most of all Michaels was known for not tolerating anything less than perfection. When the Washington bureau chief was unable to answer a question about a story one of his reporters had written, Michaels calmly got up from his desk, took a cab to LaGuardia, hopped on the next shuttle flight to Washington and fired the entire bureau—on Christmas Eve.

This was Paul's new boss.

Now, even though Paul didn't know the first thing about business, he thought he knew a lot about writing. After all, his articles had been featured prominently almost every day on the "Woman's Page" (as the style or food sections used to be known) of *The Star-Ledger*.

And so, outfitted in suits of the finest polyester, Paul set off to write articles for the magazine about companies that made beer, tires, or something called the "personal computer."

The first stories Paul wrote had long, flowing, Faulkneresque sentences—filled with description and asides. He was thoroughly impressed with himself.

After reading the 4th such article—this one about a supermarket chain in the Midwest—Michaels had had it. He threw open his office door and yelled in a voice that people swore they could hear 2 blocks away, "Brown! Get in here!

"You think readers are hanging on your every word, don't you?" Michaels fumed as he held Paul's latest story at arm's length as if it were an old tuna fish sandwich gone bad. "Well, let me tell you a little about your reader. He's a guy who has just put in a hard day at the office; something didn't go well.

"He goes home, hoping to have a drink, but the moment he walks in the door, his wife is yelling at him about what the kids did. He gets exactly 5 minutes before dinner to pick up the magazine, and the last thing he is going to do is wade through your prose [if sarcasm could actually drip off a word, it would have here]. He just wants to know if he should buy stock in this [expletive deleted] supermarket chain or not."

Paul sat silently, stunned. No one, not even the evil Mrs. Gawe in 6th grade, had ever found fault with anything he had written. And worse yet, Michaels was not only criticizing his writing—he was calling into question Paul's entire approach to writing.

"You ever read any Hemingway?" Michaels asked, before the shock wore off.

"No."

"Alright, tomorrow, Wednesday, don't come into work. Get a Hemingway book and read it. I want to see you first thing Thursday and you are going to tell me what you learned. Now, get out of here!"

Even Paul, whose taste in fiction begins and ends with murder mysteries, knew of Ernest Hemingway, the Nobel prize–winning novelist (1899-1961) who wrote such classics as *The Sun Also Rises* and *A Farewell to Arms*. But Paul had spent his college career taking a strange mix of drama,

history, and mathematics courses, so he missed the twenti-
eth century literature classes that would have steeped him
in Hemingway.

On Wednesday, Paul went to a bookstore and bought
the shortest Hemingway novel he could find—*The Old
Man and the Sea*—and started reading:

> **He was an old man who fished alone in a skiff
> on the Gulf Stream and had gone eighty-four
> days now without taking a fish. In the first
> forty days a boy had been with him. But after
> forty days without a fish the boy's parents had
> told him that the old man was now definitely
> and finally salao, which is the worst form of
> unlucky, and the boy had gone at their orders
> in another boat, which caught three good fish
> the first week.**

By page 4, Paul realized Michaels didn't want a book
report about an old man, fishing, and the sea. As he continued to read the tale about an old Cuban fisherman, down
on his luck, and his battle with a giant marlin, Paul thought
about what Hemingway's writing had to do with an article
about a supermarket chain.

First thing on Thursday, Paul appeared at Michaels'
door. "Okay, I get it," Paul said. "It's all about the story,
which has a beginning, middle, and end. Short sentences;
active verbs. Words shouldn't distract from the narrative.
They need to drive it forward."

Michaels nodded once. "Go do that from now on. Now,
get out of here!"

From that day forward, all of Paul's work—whether short magazine pieces or long, complex business books—told a story. The sentences became shorter. Verbs drove the action forward. Adjectives were used sparingly and only when absolutely necessary.

It's not Hemingway, but it's a living.

7 | Provide easy navigation

Since your audience members don't have time to search for information, it's essential that you provide them with an easy way to find what they're looking for. You need to create simple navigation that lets them access communication according to their needs. In this chapter we will show you how.

HERE'S A LOVELY FANTASY: You've won a 2-week, all-expenses-paid vacation at a luxury island resort. You and your significant other are staying in a beachside villa that is a 5-minute stroll from the resort's main compound, where the restaurant, pool, boat harbor, dive shop, and other amenities are located. Next to the resort is a nature preserve with walking trails and lagoons for snorkeling. Just down the road a mile or so is the charming village, which has more restaurants, great shopping, and lively bars.

Since you have no agenda and unlimited time, you don't need a watch or a map. Every morning you get up and (eventually) decide what to do that day. Sometimes you hit the beach, other times you take a leisurely stroll. You explore. You wander. If you go the long way or even get a little lost, it doesn't matter.

Remember, though, this is a fantasy.

Unfortunately, back in the real world, most of us are so pressed for time that we are always looking for the shortest route. Before we begin our morning commute, we listen to the radio traffic report. We consult MapQuest (hoping it will be accurate) when planning a trip to an unfamiliar place. We race into the supermarket, scanning the signs to find the aisle for jalapeño peppers. We park near the mall entrance that's closest to the store we need. And, when it comes to finding information, we also seek the shortest route. We don't have the time to meander or the patience to lose ourselves in communication. We want to get in, get done, and get out.

Here's what this means to you: To appeal to your audience, you must give them easy access to the information you're providing. The front door has to be clearly visible, the hallways clean, the aisles clearly labeled, the products at eye level, and the exit signs always brightly illuminated. If your audience members start to feel overwhelmed or confused, they won't muddle through—they'll get out as fast as their legs can carry them.

The patron saint of navigation

Christopher Columbus, Vasco de Gama, and Henry Hudson were okay at exploring, but for our money, the greatest navigator of all time is Al Neuharth. Never heard of him? Mr. Neuharth didn't make it into our navigation hall of fame by wandering around the world in a wooden boat: He's the poor country boy from South Dakota who built the nation's largest newspaper company, Gannett, and created *USA Today*.

Ah, *USA Today*. So simple, so humble, and yet so brilliant. When it made its debut in 1982, *USA Today* was denigrated for being too lowbrow. The idea that a serious newspaper would be colorful (literally) with short articles and bite-sized information was heretical to communication professionals (especially writers and journalists and everyone else in love with long narrative copy). They dubbed *USA Today* "McPaper" and derided it as being "Paper Lite."

Then, the next day—well, within a couple of months, to be precise—they started to imitate it.

Why "navigation"?

We use the term "navigation" to describe the idea of making information accessible because we think it is the best term to describe the experience of finding one's way through any type of communication: print, electronic, even a PowerPoint presentation. Webster's dictionary defines "navigate" as "to direct a course," and we think that is a good description of what we do for a living. As communicators, it's our job to help our audience quickly and easily traverse the information we're providing.

Newspapers that had been a sea of gray suddenly discovered color. Magazines that were strictly linear became more modular. When news Web sites (cnn.com, washingtonpost.com, etc.) were created a few years later, their homepages looked suspiciously like the front page of *USA Today*. (More than 20 years later, most still do.)

The secret to *USA Today*'s success was, and is, simple: The newspaper honors its readers, respects the fact that they have limited time and attention, and likes readers just as they are.

So many "established" newspapers seem to be like a judgmental spouse, saying they love you, but then wanting you to apply yourself, be more attentive, straighten up. *USA Today* doesn't do that. It doesn't care if readers are distracted and messy. It knows that we're just as interested in Jennifer Aniston as we are in the Federal Reserve (actually, more interested, but that's our little secret). It wants to help us find information quickly and easily, and have fun doing it. In short, *USA Today* is a good role model for any communication, and it's especially valuable when thinking about how to make your communication easier to navigate.

USA Today explained

What makes *USA Today*'s navigation so effective? Here are just a few ingredients:

- **It's organized by topic.** The newspaper has 4 separate sections identified by color: News is blue, Sports is red, Money is green, Life is purple. Don't like sports? Find the section with the red tab. Lift it out and move on.
- **Color** is also used as a key throughout the entire paper to help readers identify and find information. On the front page in the left-hand summary column called "Newsline," each story is marked with a little color-coded box (green is financial; blue is for news, etc.) to indicate what type of information it contains.
- **Layout**—through placement and length—makes it clear which article is most important, which is second, which is third, and so forth. Ever read an archived newspaper from 40 years ago? In most issues, everything was the same size and prominence, so it was hard to tell where to look first. *USA Today* leverages the

The trouble with text

Narrative copy—long strings of sentences, separated only by indented new paragraphs—may be fine in a novel, but these days, unbroken text doesn't work in any other venue (including a book like this one). Wading through sentence after sentence after sentence after sentence just seems like too much work. There's no access point and no alternative—you have no choice but to start at the beginning and hope you can stay awake long enough to get to the end. Good navigation removes the psychological barrier. If the communication looks like something that requires "a quick read" rather than a major investment of time and attention, we're more likely to give it a try.

article's placement (higher up on the page means it is more important), the size of the headline (the bigger it is, the more the editors want you to pay attention), whether or not a photo or illustration is included, and other graphic elements to guide the reader.

- **Information is cross-referenced.** Every section has a summary in the left-hand column ("Newsline," "Sportsline," "Moneyline," and, our favorite, "Lifeline") that allows readers to quickly get the gist of what's covered. To help readers find the full story, each summary contains the corresponding page number.

- **It's not linear.** Before *USA Today*, most newspaper editors made the assumption that their publications would be read in an orderly fashion, from front to back. (Readers actually didn't read that way, but that didn't concern the editors.) *USA Today* recognized that busy readers—especially travelers that are its core audience—wanted to skim and skip at will. If a story continues to another page—and very few of them do—it always concludes within the section where it started. You will never see a news article ending in the life section.

- **Headlines, subheads, and sidebars** are used to break up copy, punctuate important points, and draw the reader into and through each story. And typography techniques—size, style, lightness, or boldness—are employed as both a graphic and a navigational tool. (See Chapter 8 for more on typography.)

"The paragraph is too poorly defined to be a basic unit of analysis."

Stanford Professor Robert E. Horn

Navigation and the geeks

The ancient Greeks learned to navigate by looking at the stars. The modern geeks discovered navigation by staring at the computer screen. The geeks realized that Web sites and other complex electronic systems had the potential to contain so much stuff that, unless there were logical ways to organize and package the information, it would become an impenetrable mess.

That's why information technology professionals—and their colleagues in academia—developed an overlapping (and sometimes contradictory) set of disciplines: information design. Information mapping. Structured writing.

The concept behind all of these is the same. As Robert E. Horn, a consultant and visiting scholar at Stanford University, writes, "Information design is defined as the art and science of preparing information so that it can be used by human beings with efficiency and effectiveness." In other words, it's about organizing and packaging information to make it easy to access and use.

The foundation for information design is structured writing, which "provides a systematic way of analyzing any subject matter to be conveyed in a written document," according to Mr. Horn. "It consists of a set of techniques for analyzing, organizing, sequencing, and displaying the various units of information."

But organizing information is just the beginning. In its fully realized form, information design creates a complete integration of content, structure, and visuals. Picture a recipe that not only conveys ingredients and techniques in words, but illustrates every one. Or a manual on how to use a machine that includes written description, mathematical formulas, demonstration illustrations, and all other pertinent information, so you can know exactly what to do and how to do it.

Sound too theoretical or too complicated to be useful? You don't need to have a Ph.D. or a pocket protector to put the concept of information design to work. The idea is to approach your communication not as an undefined blob of tofu but as a collection of information that can be logically organized so that the audience can easily navigate through it.

How do you get started? To make navigation simpler, there are 7 essential elements you should consider using. They will add structure and focus to your communication:

7 essential navigational elements

Where to find them in this chapter:

1. What's-ahead contents

For virtually every communication Alison's firm creates for clients—from 4-paragraph e-mails to 20-slide Power-Point presentations to 50-page handbooks—a contents list is included up front. That's because people want to know what's inside or what's ahead, to help them decide how to navigate and/or participate.

For example, recently members of Alison's team were helping a health care company communicate organizational change to its employees. An e-mail memo from a divisional president had to be long enough to contain significant content, but that meant it couldn't be read quickly on just a single screen. By starting with a bulleted contents list, the e-mail became easier to navigate. Here's an excerpt:

MEMO

Dear Colleagues:

I'd like to share the progress we've made in building the new organization. We still have a lot of hard work ahead of us, but we're beginning to see the new structure take shape.

In the following paragraphs, I'll tell you about:

> *Where you can learn more about organizational improvement efforts*

> *How our new structure supports the company's new strategy*

> *What progress we've made on staffing the new organization*

> *How we're working to improve processes*

Where you can learn more

The leadership team is committed to communicating the organization's progress as we move forward. But so much is happening so fast that, quite frankly, it's a challenge to keep communication current and complete. So, in addition to communicating via meetings and overview messages like this one, we are building a dedicated intranet site that will be launched on March 1, which will be updated frequently with information about how the strategy is being implemented.

[The e-mail continued, following the same structure, for three more paragraphs.]

 PAGE NUMBERS

A contents list is made even more valuable by including page numbers (in print) or links (on a Web site). As Richard Saul Wurman, author of *Information Anxiety,* says, "It was something like 26 years after the first Gutenberg Bible that somebody invented pagination. Page numbers allow you access; it was one of the first steps in trying to understand things and find things."

2. Quick-read summary

Remember "executive summaries"? The idea was that senior managers were much too busy (or was it really that they were too ditsy?) to read an entire report or proposal. That meant that in order to get senior managers to pay attention and to relay the essence of what you wanted to convey, you needed to create a brief summary of the content.

Since a lack of attention has now become a universal problem, a quick-read summary now makes sense for almost every audience—especially if your content is longer than a page (or a screen).

Summaries should not be clever; the idea is to capture the gist of what the entire report, article, brochure, or other content means to convey, not to show off your IQ or wit.

Although you'd love your audience to absorb the communication in its entirety—and the summary should certainly sell the value of the whole piece—it's better to get

Navigation as a competitive advantage

It's a paradox: So much data is available, yet it's such a challenge to find the specific information you need right now to solve a problem or get work done. According to a 2005 study by research firm Outsell, today's professionals spend 53 percent of their time seeking out information, 7 percent more than they did in 2001. Add it all up, and it means that in U.S. corporations, professionals spend 5.4 billion hours a year trying to find information. This is worth noting because it's an opportunity for those of us who try to communicate. If we can make our information very clear and easy to navigate (like, say, *USA Today*), it will not only stand out, it will provide a service to all those busy people we're trying to reach.

Smart summaries

Many magazines use quick-read summaries in their contents pages these days to help readers learn what is contained inside and encourage them to read individual articles. When they work well—as these examples from the November 2005 issue of *Runner's World* demonstrate—summaries capture the essence of the content while promoting the benefits of reading the entire article:

BEGINNERS

Overuse injuries are a common problem for new runners. These simple strategies will help you prevent them before they start. PLUS: Learn how to gauge your running progress without racing.

TRAIN YOUR BRAIN

Fast feet will take you only so far. To do your best in a race, you've got to be mentally tough, too. Here's how to prime your mind for competition in any distance.

NATURE'S BEST RECOVERY FOODS

Potassium helps keep you hydrated and aids in recovery. And, since it's found in lots of delicious, everyday foods, you won't have a problem getting plenty of it. Check out our favorite sources.

a few minutes of the audience's attention than none at all. In other words, even if they only read the summary, you're ahead of the game.

3. Top-down structure (the inverted pyramid)

The "once upon a time" structure, where the plot proceeds in a leisurely fashion as if it's meandering through the forest while the audience is carried along, not knowing where the path will lead or even how long the journey will be, is great for bedtime stories. But for most other communication, the audience doesn't have the patience to wander.

The inverted pyramid explained

Here's an easy way to understand the inverted pyramid, according to Ken Blake, Ph.D., associate professor of journalism at Middle Tennessee State University. Picture an upside-down triangle, with a broad base on the top and the narrow tip on the bottom. "The broad base represents the most newsworthy information. . . . The narrow tip represents the least newsworthy information," Mr. Blake writes. When you write using the inverted pyramid format, you put the most important information at the beginning and the least important information at the end. For more information, see Mr. Blake's very useful overview on the inverted pyramid at *http://mtsu32.mtsu .edu:11178/171/pyramid.htm.*

They need to get the most important information—the main point or the punch line—almost immediately.

As a result, the best structure for most communication is a classic: the inverted pyramid.

Anyone who's taken a journalism course is familiar with the inverted pyramid. Legend has it that the inverted pyramid came into use in the days of the telegraph, when unreliable service meant that if you wanted to make sure you got your message through, you put the most important information at the beginning. In any case, the inverted pyramid came into general use in journalism in the mid-nineteenth century and remains the standard.

Today, the inverted pyramid's greatest advantage is that it helps your audience members decide how they want to use your content. They simply stop reading when they run out of time (or interest), certain that they learned the key points.

" On average, five times as many people read the headline as read the body copy. It follows that unless your headline sells your product, you have wasted 90 percent of your money. **"**

Advertising legend David Ogilvy in his book Ogilvy on Advertising

Most Newsworthy/Important

THE INVERTED
PYRAMID

Least Newsworthy/Important

Although the inverted pyramid had somewhat fallen into disfavor for being too staid, it has had a comeback with Web writers, who know that the most important information has to be first, since only the most interested Web site visitor scrolls down past the first screen.

One reason we find the inverted pyramid useful is that it disciplines you to order information according to priority. The process of deciding what's really important, what's slightly less important, and so on, requires you to think about what's important to the audience.

4. Helpful headlines

No aspect of communication is more important than the headline. The headline is the first thing the audience notices. It grabs their attention. It promises the solution to their problem or question. At its very best, a headline addresses the most important question of all, "What's in it for me?"

If headlines are so important, why didn't we devote an entire chapter to headlines? Why isn't this whole book about headlines?

The reason is simple: Headlines aren't that hard. We believe that good headlines are simply common sense. They're logical. They shouldn't be overly clever—no word-play, no alliteration, no rhyming, no limericks—just simple, short, and straightforward.

Today's audience doesn't want cute or clever. These folks are in a hurry and want the headline to tell them exactly what the communication is about—so they can make a quick decision about whether or not to spend time with it.

Lots of people have advice about headlines—especially advertising experts—and there are many courses on copywriting that also focus on how to write headlines. We recommend you keep one thing in mind when writing headlines: Focus on the needs of your audience. What are audience members interested in? What do they need to know? How can you write a headline that will solve a problem or answer a burning question? If you accomplish that, your headline will be successful. (See Chapter 2 for more on how to understand and meet your audience's needs.)

Write your headline before you create content

There is a technique to help you write headlines that meet your audience's needs: Before you start shaping your communication, write the headline. Ask yourself: What is the most important point you want to communicate to your readers? Once you've identified this high concept (see Chapter 4), write your headline to capture it, explaining exactly what your communication is about.

One mistake many people make is writing the headline *after* they've finished creating the communication. This is dangerous because you're writing the headline from the perspective of someone who already knows every detail, thus making it tempting to write a "clever" headline that doesn't really tell what the story is about.

Here's an example. An employee publication for a large bank contained the headline, "Lighting the Way."

What is the story about? You can't tell from the headline. In fact, the article describes a loan the bank made to an electric company. "Lighting the way" . . . get it? But only after you've read the story does the headline make sense.

 3 HEADLINES

For our money, there are three types of headline that work best:

Make a promise. "Reduce your energy costs by 14 percent."

Ask a question. "How much would you spend for peace of mind?"

Tell "how to." "How to get promoted" or "12 ways to talk to your teenager."

Now, let's say you sat down and asked yourself before writing the story: What is the most important point? Obviously, that the bank lent the electric company a certain amount of money. Since that's the main point, it should also be the headline: "ICG Bank lends Ucorp $250,000."

You could use a subhead to provide details: "Electric company will use the loan to expand into new neighborhoods." By the time readers are finished reading the head, they can make an educated decision about whether or not they need to read on.

5. Subheads and breakheads

If the headline is the star of your communication show, subheads—the secondary, more detailed copy lines that accompany the headlines—and breakheads—the bold-faced subtitles that define sections of content—are the supporting cast. Major magazines like *BusinessWeek* are masters at using headlines, subheads, and breakheads to draw audience members in and provide them with useful information. Here's an example from the October 31, 2005, issue:

Type of headline	Subject matter (Article about new Sears CEO)	Purpose of headline
Section heading	"People"	Describes the section of the magazine
Headline	"At Sears, A Great Communicator"	Attracts the reader and draws him/her in
Subhead	"New CEO Lewis will need his people skills to overhaul the giant's hidebound culture"	Summarizes what the story is about

Here's another example, this from the November 26, 2005, issue of *The Economist:*

Type of headline	Subject matter (Article on the U.S. involvement in Iraq)	Purpose of headline
Section heading	"The United States"	Describes the content section
Headline	"Not whether, but how, to withdraw"	Draws the reader in
Subhead	"As the war in Iraq grows ever less popular, new thinking at last is in the air"	Summarizes what the story is about

This is a breakhead

Breakheads "break up" long unrelieved blocks of paragraphs and allow the audience to move through information more quickly, since members can skip from place to place instead of having to slog through sentence by sentence, step by tiring step.

There's a school of thought—which we subscribe to—in communication circles these days that in any communication piece you create, headlines should get the audience started, subheads help the audience understand what the communication is about, and breakheads provide all the highlights (even if you don't read every word of the narrative).

We think this makes sense in today's overloaded world. After all, don't you want people to get the message, even if they have only a few minutes to spend on your e-mail, brochure, or other communication?

6. At-a-glance sidebars

Remember our premise: People don't have the time or patience to process long content crammed with information. One way to get your message across is to break out a portion of your narrative into sidebars: self-contained sections (such as checklists, tables, annotated illustrations or other formats) that amplify points you make in your main text.

Sidebars have long been a staple of newspaper and magazine writing. For example, some years ago, Paul wrote a

Navigation creates choice

There are many reasons why it's important to make your communication easy to navigate. Here's another: People increasingly expect to control their communication experiences—they want to choose what to pay attention to, based on their personal interests. This need for choice is explained by media strategist David DeSocio, from global communications company OMD. To illustrate how choice is a way of life for most people, Mr. DeSocio offers these fun facts about TV in 2005:

- The average TV viewer changes channels 8,000 times a week.
- There are only 18 TV shows with an average Nielsen rating of 5.0 or higher. That means there are only 18 television shows a week that get more than 5 percent of America to tune in. By contrast, 1,723 shows deliver less than a 1.0 rating.
- The number 1 show for kids is not *SpongeBob SquarePants* or, in fact, any other kids-oriented show you could think of—it's the Super Bowl, the same TV event that's number 1 for virtually every other demographic. In fact, the Super Bowl is now one of the few television experiences that is universal across ages, genders, and ethnic groups.

Interesting stuff to amuse (or bore) your friends, but what does it all mean? According to Mr. DeSocio, these facts demonstrate the personalization of media. "People don't watch TV. They don't listen to radio. And they don't read magazines. What do they do? They make personal choices," he said. And that feeling of choice sets expectations for the way people approach all communication.

YOUR ATTENTION, PLEASE.

magazine article on Maker's Mark bourbon that described the company's unique approach to marketing. The premise of the article was clearly conveyed in the headline and subhead:

How to Host the Perfect Weekend
OK, not just any weekend—Kentucky Derby Weekend. Here's how Maker's Mark CEO Bill Samuels mixes business with pleasure, turns guests into friends, and converts customers into missionaries. (Hint: the bourbon helps.)

Even though his editors gave him plenty of space, there were still significant bits of information—a "how to" component, and a bit more "color" that he wanted to include. And so he wrote two sidebars—"Party Tricks" (*see following page*) and "A Weekend at Billy's."

7. Laundry-list bullets

Our last navigation suggestion is about bullets. Rather than going on and on, sentence after sentence, paragraph after paragraph, gray page after gray page, use bullets and their cousins, check marks and numbered lists, to break things up. Whether used as a sidebar ("here are the 5 things you need to know about the company's new initiative") or as part of the main text, bullets are a wonderful way to:

- Separate important information from the rest of the text.
- Underscore key points.
- Break up long narrative text naturally.
- Give readers a natural entry point into whatever it is you have to write.

 BULLETS

Use bullets judiciously; if everything is a list, it all blurs together and your audience's brains begin to fry.

Simply a sidebar

Here's an excerpt of one of the sidebars Paul created for the Maker's Mark article:

PARTY TRICKS

Bill Samuels has been hosting "Derby Weekend" for 35 years. Here are the most important things he's learned along the way:

1. **Stuffy is bad.** Everything from Samuels's tacky costumes to his choice of entertainment is selected with one thought in mind: Make sure his guests feel comfortable and relaxed. "The whole idea is to create an environment where people will talk to people they don't know."

2. **Set the tone from the outset.** This is an event. Guests are supposed to have fun. The only thing that is expected from them is that they come for a good time. That's communicated starting with the invitation.

3. **Track the RSVPs.** You want to know who is coming. Not only do you want to make sure that you will have enough food and drink, tickets, and accommodations, but also that you don't have too many sourpusses among your guests. All your hard work goes out the window if you end up hosting a disproportionate number of stiffs.

4. **Sweat the details.** People won't have a good time if there aren't enough bathrooms, if they're wearing the wrong shoes, or if they have to worry about anything. Samuels sets up his outdoor tents a week in advance to make sure the ground won't be soggy from any pre-event rains. And he has (prepaid) taxis standing by after the Thursday party in the of-course-unlikely event that anyone overindulges.

5. **Include a glamour component.** Mingling with—or at least ogling—celebrities is fun. Samuels's guest list always includes a handful of actors, athletes, and musicians.

(➡) INSIGHT 7:
You are here

There's a fascinating book called *Why We Buy: The Science of Shopping* by Paco Underhill that explains how retailers and others use a variety of tested techniques to get you to (1) put that item in your cart and (2) buy it.

These techniques include everything from lighting and signage to physical layout to whether or not they even have shopping carts (Target does; Macy's doesn't), and why.

What does shopping have to do with communication? Everything. Retailers survive only because they can attract their customers' attention and persuade them to make a purchase.

We believe anyone who communicates—who needs to "sell" your audience on spending time with our message—can learn a lot by shopping. (Actually, Alison believes that shopping is not only educational, but therapeutic, but that's a different story.)

And one thing retailers do very well is help shoppers navigate, to find what they need when they need it. While it's true that stores would like everyone to browse for hours, touching everything and trying on every other item, they know that most customers are pressed for time.

Companies that want you to buy their stuff understand that they have to create an environment (physical or virtual) where you can easily find the item, enjoy doing so, touch it/smell it/taste it/visualize it, try it on, and take it with you when it's time to go.

But when it comes to communication, people often feel dazed and confused. They don't see the value of each communication channel, don't know how things are organized or how they fit together, and can't easily find the information they're looking for. For your audience, it's like being stuck at an endless checkout line in some now-defunct retailer that deserved to die: Bradlees. Caldor. The Wiz. Ames department stores.

What's the problem? Communication is confusing and complex, and people need to be reminded how the system works—how to get around the store. Think mall map: "You are here. This is where you find the food court."

The advantage, of course, is that if you help people find what they're looking for, they're likely to buy it.

The latest fashion: choice

All this talk about malls and stores is making us (well, at least Alison) think about fashion. If you understand an important fashion phenomenon, it will help you communicate more effectively. It's not about pencil skirts or ponchos, it's about something bigger and more pervasive: personal choice.

What to do differently

✓ Make your communication easy to navigate, giving your audience control of the experience.

✓ Don't use long blocks of narrative text—it will seem to your audience like too much work and too much of a commitment.

✓ Look at *USA Today* for inspiration; emulate the way the newspaper organizes content and makes it accessible.

✓ Employ all 7 elements of navigation described in this chapter: contents, summary, inverted pyramid, headlines, subheads/breakheads, sidebars, and bullets.

✓ Use checklists like this one.

The *Wall Street Journal* reported on this trend in 2004 ("As Consumers Mix and Match, Fashion Industry Starts to Fray"), but it's actually been occurring for several years in stores, which is where fashion really takes place. Rather than buying an entire look or "outfit"—top, skirt or pants, jacket—from one designer or clothing maker, women are cherry-picking the items they like best, then mixing them with other disparate pieces from their existing wardrobe or from other designers. (The trend extends to men, too, but they're much less of an economic force in fashion.)

How does this relate to communication? The *Journal*'s reporter Teri Agins draws a connection: "The effect on fashion is similar to what's happening whenever technology has zapped the authority of cultural arbiters. Consumers' newfound freedom to customize their lives—from burning their own music CDs to publishing political commentary online—is throwing basic business models of many businesses into disarray."

Keep following the thread and you'll see how communication is connected. Consumers have gotten used to controlling the experience—to making news (personalized portals), entertainment (iPod), and fashion their own. Yet too often communication only comes in one size: one access point, organizing principle, type of information. That's the equivalent of saying that the only shirts available are black, short-sleeved, size 10. That's bad fashion and even worse communication.

8 | Make it visual

Visuals are a no-fail way to grab and hold people's attention. But you don't need to have artistic ability—or a graphic designer on retainer—to use visuals to turn boring narrative into compelling content. We'll show you how anyone (even us writers) can do it.

IMAGINE A WINDING ROAD on a dark night in a foreign country. You're in a borrowed car with slippery steering, dim headlights, and questionable brakes. You try to drive carefully, but you have to get down the mountain in time to save the damsel in distress, stop the bank from foreclosing, or tell him how you really feel before he departs forever.

The roadside has many signs, indicating the angle of the curves ahead, warning about deer crossing, communicating the speed limit. But your headlights are so dim, and your eyes are so focused on the pavement, that you barely see the signs. Suddenly an especially large one looms ahead: It shows a picture of a bridge with a large red slash through it. There are some words, too, but you don't speak the language. Your distracted brain suddenly engages, and you think, "Bridge out?" Rounding a turn, you hit the brakes and screech to a stop, inches from a precipice where the bridge used to be.

Saved by a visual.

(Don't worry: You get down the mountain in time. A farmer with a mule appears, or an old friend just happens by in his helicopter, or you discover an old dirt road. You make it. You rescue the damsel. The foreclosure is stopped. He agrees not to leave. You all live happily ever after.)

Here's the point: Whether your audience is racing down a mountain or sitting at their computers, they're so overwhelmed by content that mere words won't get their attention. You need to write less (more on that in Chapter 9) and use more visuals to effectively convey your message.

In this chapter, we'll provide you with the essentials on communicating visually. Obviously, there's a lot more you could learn—institutions of higher learning like the School of Visual Arts and Rhode Island School of Design offer degrees in the subject—but this will get you started.

The importance of visuals

We all have a preferred learning style: hearing, seeing, or doing. Most adults respond to visuals and are visual learners. Visuals are also important because they:

- **Can tell a whole story at a glance, faster, and with greater nuance than words.** (There is a reason that

What is a visual?

We use the term "visual" as a noun because we think it bests describes anything that illustrates a concept, rather than conveying it in words alone. A visual can be:

The way text or typography is used can be a visual. For example, putting something in **boldface**, *italics*, or shadow creates a visual effect. Different **fonts** or tyPe SizEs qualify, too. (Please don't try this at home.)

Colors

Graphic elements, such as icons

Charts, graphs, and tables

Illustrations, either original or clip art

Diagrams

Photographs

Maps

Cartoons/Animation

Filmed images (movies, television, commercials, etc.)

the cliché "A picture's worth a 1,000 words" exists. It's true.) We are all busy—now more than ever. Your audience wants access to information that is fast and easy to digest and understand. Visuals support the need to "get it" fast.

- **Are memorable.** When we attach a visual to an important message, it creates recall. We can help people remember messages by giving them visual "handles" to grasp when trying to recall content. A study by the Wharton Research Center at the University of Pennsylvania showed that, in presentations, when information is only conveyed orally, people only retain 10 percent of the content. But when a presentation includes visuals and words, retention increases to 50 percent.

- **Make the complicated simple.** Got a complex message you need to communicate? The more technical and multilayered the concept is, the more you need visuals to create interest and understanding. Whether you're communicating about an intricate process change or presenting complicated data, visuals can simplify your ideas and make it quick and easy for the audience to grasp information.

◀◀ The more technical and multilayered the concept is, the more you need visuals to create interest and understanding.

3 simple ways to use visuals

We're going to share 3 easy-to-do ways to begin putting visuals to work for you: Jazz up typography, embrace icons, and get colorful.

Of course, this chapter is just the beginning. In virtually every situation, a photograph, cartoon, map, or even a simple table can enhance your message and get it across with more power.

1. Use typography to add visual interest

A number of roadblocks prevent us from making communication more visual: lack of time, a strained budget, limited access to professional designers, etc. As a result, we're often left with a sea of copy that people are likely to ignore. But you have more control than you realize to get attention. Using just text, you can create visual interest. Here's how.

The ABCs (and DEs) of making type more visual

It's time to make friends with your formatting palette; apply these methods to Word documents, PowerPoint presentations, and e-mail to get your messages noticed.

A. Use more than one typeface. Varying your font is a good way to create visual contrast. Perhaps the most important rule of good typography is don't overdo it. The standard is no more than 2 fonts per article: It's tempting to go nuts and make a crazy quilt of typeface styles, but that only looks messy, not appealing.

B. Make headlines and subheads bold. As we described in Chapter 7, headlines and subheads create navigation, indicating the hierarchy of your content. They act as starting cues indicating where sections begin and what the sections are about. Therefore, headlines and subheads should always be clearly visible. Try boldface, 2 or more point sizes bigger than your text. If your body text is a serif (type where a smaller line is used to finish off the main stroke of a letter, as on the top and bottom of this letter "**M**") try using a sans-serif for the headline or vice versa. (This is what a

⚠ TYPOGRAPHY

"Typography" is the balance and interplay of text that helps readers understand, absorb, and navigate content. Page after page of dense text makes it hard for readers to cut through the thicket. But when type is used well, there is a balance—among blocks of text, headlines or subheads, and the surrounding white space—that draws readers in.

sans-serif "M" looks like.) If you're using all the same font style, make headlines and subheads a different color.

C. Vary your typestyles. Use your formatting palette to emphasize words or an important sentence. **Bold** and *italic*, used together or separately, attract the eye. In a block of text, they help employees navigate the content, acting as road signs and suggesting importance. Making key words and phrases bold is an effective way to break up the monotony of straight text.

D. Paint your article with a little bit of color. Color isn't just for headlines. If there is a paragraph or 2 that you want to call attention to, apply a legible color that offers enough contrast from the rest of the text but can still be read

These darn kids!

If you're communicating to anyone under age 32, you've simply got to use visuals. The younger (and especially the youngest) generations have grown up in a world where visual is the norm. Think about their experiences and complete comfort with:

    TV, everywhere

    Movies that you can watch almost anywhere—in a theater, at home, on the computer

    Video games (movies that you play)

    Computer-generated animation

    Cell phones that take photos, play video clips, allow you to play games and surf the Web

    And, of course, the Internet

against the background (i.e., blue, red, or burgundy against a white background). Test legibility by making a photocopy of your page. If your colored text is too light, go for a darker color. Find a sentence that sums up your objective and make it 4 to 6 points bigger than your body font size. Make sure to leave adequate white space around the sentence (put in a

A is for alphabet

To a young child, the letter "A" is abstract; it doesn't stand for anything. As Paul Martin Lester, professor at California State University at Fullerton, writes in his article "Syntactic Theory of Visual Communication, Part One," it's not until a child begins to match up letters with the words they represent that the abstract shapes A, B, C, and so on begin to mean anything. "Before we are four years old, most of us learned The Alphabet Song," writes Mr. Lester. "Sung to the same tune of "Twinkle Twinkle Little Star," it is unlike any song because no pictures come to mind when singing it. With Twinkle, we can look up in the night's sky and imagine a little star out of the billions shining just for us. But a song about the letters in the alphabet does not carry any visual equivalents."

For a child, it only begins to make sense as the letters become associated with the concrete: "A is for apple, B is for bear . . ." Mr. Lester explains, "Each letter of the alphabet becomes a picture that corresponds with a complex set of direct and mediated images. We no longer have to think of an actual red, juicy apple. We can simply see the letter 'A' and know that it stands for the fruit."

But even when we become fully literate—immersed in words, awash in them, and able to use them to describe nearly anything—we continue to have a connection with the images we started with as children. Psychologists have discovered that concrete nouns—apple, bear, chair—are easier to remember than abstract ones (such as abstract, baseless, or careful) because of their link to real objects.

Words help us understand, but we'd really rather look at the pictures.

box if you are feeling creative) and voila! You've got yourself a callout.

E. Use all-capitalized text as a call to action. But a word to the wise: Use this device sparingly. Large blocks of text set in all caps are uncomfortable to read and can slow reading. It can also be construed as conveying anger. Use all caps for short statements to MAKE A MESSAGE SHOUT. Limited to a short call to action, headlines, or subheads, all caps can be effective.

2. Embrace eye-catching icons

Icons are so prevalent in our day-to-day lives that we often don't even notice them as communication. For example, we intrinsically recognize that when a door has an image of a figure wearing a dress, it communicates that on the other side is the women's bathroom.

Since one simple graphic demonstrates a concept that would take many words to explain, icons can be a particularly powerful communication tool.

Here's what makes icons so effective:

- **They're widely applicable.** A well-designed icon has the same meaning globally, offering a rich potential for communicating across language barriers. For example, let's say that safety is a corporate priority for your organization; an icon of a hardhat would be universally understood.
- **They cut through the clutter.** Between all the words in print and online, an icon stands out like a beacon in the night to help the audience navigate, guiding them

CALLOUTS

Callouts (sometimes called a "pull quote") pull a sentence or 2 out of the copy—usually in the margins of the text—and frame or highlight them in a different color. It's an easy editorial design method, used often in magazines, and an effective way to break up copy and make key points easy to reference.

ICONS

An icon is a small, easy-to-recognize image that (if well-designed) is universally understood. An icon becomes shorthand for an idea or concept. Most icons are one-dimensional and one color, and their style can vary from realistic to abstract.

to various kinds of content. On a subscription Web site, a "key" icon represents premium content, so if you're a member, you'll be able to access in-depth content.

- **They create recall.** Some organizations use icons to represent important information, like company values. Icons serve as "handles" that people can grasp when trying to recall information. Used consistently, icons reinforce messages and further emphasize their importance. When used with written content, icons can also create clarity by linking to overarching concepts.

How to use icons
When creating your own icons—follow these guidelines:

- **Make sure they're clear.** Only very simple images make a good icon. If you're icon is too busy visually, you run the risk that your audience won't be able to make out the image, which is especially problematic if the icon is reduced for use on a Web page or becomes hard to read when a document it is used on is photocopied.
- **Ensure that they're without cultural bias.** Colors and images vary from culture to culture. For example, in France, an icon of a house would not represent "homepage" because the French call it a "welcome page." Before introducing icons, test them on a diverse group of people and get feedback. Keep it simple: Too many icons can add to confusion. Don't overdo it.
- **Hire a designer.** If you need to create an icon from scratch, it may be time to invest in professional help. Think about when and where you could leverage

icons: operating principles, values, business strategies, etc. Then, enlist a designer's help. The cost is minimal and the results are worth it.

- **Make it easy for people to learn what icons mean.** Don't ever take it for granted that everyone knows what different icons represent. Whether in print or online, include a key that offers an explanation of each icon (*see figure below left*).

What's so great about clip art?

Clip art—premade icons, drawings, or other graphic elements—existed long before the invention of the computer. These images were originally compiled in books, and artists cut ("clipped") them out and pasted them onto the page. But the Internet and the electronic image has catapulted clip art to new levels—so much so that today, the Houghton Mifflin dictionary defines clip art this way: "Ready-made pieces of printed or computerized graphic art, such as illustrations, borders, and backgrounds, that can be electronically copied and used to decorate a document."

Clip art gets a bad rap because it's most often associated with corny bad cartoons or equally amateurish graphics that are sprinkled like confetti across less-than-professional-looking Web sites or desktop-published newsletters. The fact is, today's clip art can be very sophisticated and can include animations, backgrounds, banners, icons, photos, Web elements, and some professional-quality illustrations. Of course, you get what you pay for, so don't expect Van Gogh for nothing. Want to learn more about clip art? Here are 3 Web sites to check out:

www.clipart.com: More than 6 million images, available via subscription

www.clip-art.com: Links to free clip art sites

http://office.microsoft.com/clipart: You don't often associate Microsoft with art, but this site offers free images (for Office programs only, but still, free)

"We are becoming a visually mediated society. For many, understanding the world is being accomplished, not through reading words, but by reading images.**"**

Paul Martin Lester, Ph.D., professor of communication, California State University at Fullerton

3. Color it interesting

It's kind of funny, us writing about color in a black-and-white book, but we simply can't give advice on using visuals without mentioning color. (And our publisher wouldn't spring for the full-color treatment.)

Once upon a time, color was only too expensive to be widespread: Black-and-white televisions were cheaper than color TVs. Four-color brochures were substantially more expensive to print than one that used only black ink. Even more recently, you couldn't buy a color printer or a full-color screen for your cell phone, and M&Ms and washing machines came in a limited palette of colors.

But today we expect to find color wherever we go—and unless you're going for a retro look, using only black and white seems so last week.

Color it effective

Here are just a few things to remember about using color to add interest to your communication:

Color creates structure. *USA Today*, so effective at so many things, uses color well, too, as a way to create a navigation system: The front section is blue (as in "the red, white, and . . ."), the money/business section is color-coded green (of course), the sports section is red, and arts and entertainment is purple (you can draw your own conclusions about the significance of that).

Using color very sparingly can help draw attention to a particular message. In a sea of black and white, a red box immediately catches the eye. Designers often use a "burst" (splash of bright color in a box or star shape) with type to let readers know something important: "Offer expires June 1" or "One-day only sale."

Since certain colors are associated with certain concepts, using color appropriately serves as a kind of shorthand. Red means "stop," yellow "caution," green "go"—so you can color-code your communication accordingly.

When choosing colors, consider age and gender. Young children like bright, saturated, primary colors; teens like bright and saturated, too, but the color palette is subtler (teal, not plain blue, for instance). And most men simply don't like pink or purple. Take your cues about colors from fashion and top-selling products.

When to use visuals

Some situations when visuals are beneficial include:

✔ **Communicating technological system or process changes.** Visuals can also communicate what will be different, why the change is occurring, and what new behaviors are expected.

✔ **Presenting complex data.** Numbers on paper are never as effective as graphs, tables, and charts. Use visuals to tell a story and allow your audience to draw obvious conclusions. For example, if a line graph shows that employee morale is low when company productivity is low, the obvious conclusion—that low productivity = low morale—can be reached with a minimal number of words.

✔ **Reinforcing ideas and beliefs.** Corporate missions, visions, and strategies are commonly nothing more than words on paper. But creating a visual that provides insight can bring the abstract to life.

# Fun facts about color

The human eye can see 7 million colors.

Bright lemon yellow is the color that tires the eyes most quickly.

Women are more likely than men to have a favorite color.

Blue is the most popular toothbrush color in the United States.

Almost two-thirds of Americans won't buy an appliance if it doesn't come in their favorite color.

Source: J.L. Morton, color consultant, on her Web site, www.colormatters.com

INSIGHT 8:
Back to school

Remember your high school biology teacher? Alison's was a witch. Mrs. Lucas (not her real name) wasn't simply trying to teach biology—she was molding future medical students. She wanted her class to memorize all the facts about the alimentary canal for the joy of it. She thought that dissecting embalmed fetal pigs was the pinnacle of her students' existence. (Gag!)

Despite Mrs. Lucas's warped view of the world, she did have something really cool: a life-sized, 3-dimensional plastic model of a human being that started with its skin on, then could be taken apart to show the insides. (The model was a female, which caused some giggles at first, but then we got over it.) When Mrs. Lucas talked about the alimentary canal, it was easy to get confused (why is the small intestine longer than the large intestine?), but when you saw for yourself how it all worked, you got it. You didn't have to picture it. It was all right there.

Mrs. Lucas's dreams for us were partly realized (one student became a research scientist, another a physician), but most of us were too nonscientific to pursue biology as a profession.

But reflecting back on school days (or daze), lately we wonder if we should have taken a completely different path than the one Mrs. Lucas envisioned: Maybe we should have gone to film school.

This thought was stimulated by thinking about visuals in the context of an article in the *New York Times*, "Is a Cinema Studies Degree the New M.B.A.?" (March 6, 2005) by Elizabeth Van Ness.

Ms. Van Ness suggests that, if you really want to succeed in business, a film degree is more practical than an M.B.A. because film studies can be useful not only in entertainment, but also in business, politics, and any field where persuasion is key.

What to do differently

✓ Use visuals to convey your message at a glance.

✓ Don't use just pictures. Visuals include using different types of typography as well.

✓ Keep it simple. The whole idea is to make it quick and easy for your audience to grasp what you're trying to get across.

✓ Express yourself in living color. Color has (often subconscious) emotional associations. It adds impact without extra words.

"At a time when street gangs warn informers with DVD productions about the fate of 'snitches' and both terrorists and their adversaries routinely communicate in elaborately staged videos, it is not altogether surprising that film school . . . is beginning to attract those who believe that cinema isn't so much a profession as the professional language of the future," Ms. Van Ness writes.

More than 600 colleges and universities in the United States offer programs in film studies or related subjects. And since very few graduates actually become directors or producers, many students are using what they've learned to be successful in other fields.

Like, say, communication?

The article doesn't say so explicitly, but there were several thought-provoking perspectives about the power of film:

"People endowed with social power and prestige are able to use film and media images to reinforce that power—we need to look at film to grant power to those who are marginalized or currently not represented," said Rick Herbst, a graduate of the University of Notre Dame who's now at Yale Law School.

"The greatest digital divide is between those who can read and write with media, and those who can't," said Elizabeth Daley, dean of the School of Cinema-Television at the University of Southern California. U.S.C., the nation's oldest film school, believes that media competency is as fundamental as the ability to read and write. As the article reports, more than 60 general academic courses at U.S.C.

require students to create projects that use video, sound, and Internet components. Says Dean Daley, "If I had my way, our multimedia literacy honors program would be required of every student in the university."

In the digital future, words may well become secondary to images, and the greatest power in communication will reside in people who can create moving images that are retrieved via personal computer, PDA, or even cell phone.

Film school, anyone?

9 | Stay short and sweet

So little time, such fragmented attention—it's no wonder your audience needs communication that's concise and clear. This chapter will show you how to create it.

THIS SHOULD BE A NO-BRAINER: We just tell you to make your content short and simple, you do so, and we move on to the next chapter. But, for a variety of reasons, brevity is a tough challenge—and simplicity is a complex problem. Why? Because it's human nature to want to share absolutely everything we know—and it's actually easier to include the contents of the kitchen sink rather than deciding on the one point you want to make and sticking to it. (See Chapter 4 on why a single "high concept" is so important.)

The problem gets even worse if you're a subject matter expert—or if you're the one trying to help that expert convey information. Experts are chest-deep in their own knowledge, and they think the water's just fine, so they want everyone to wade in there with them. But audience members are afraid of drowning. They prefer to stay nice and dry up there on the beach rather than risk getting sucked out to sea by the undertow.

The powers that be—especially if management and lawyers are involved—feel most comfortable including every blessed fact. Clarity is risky, after all. It's much safer to include lots of clauses and disclaimers (partly because if no one can understand what the heck you're talking about, they're less likely to challenge it, or to sue).

But none of these reasons is as pernicious as good communication's worst enemy: ego. If someone (hopefully not you) is sure that he is absolutely fascinating, why wouldn't he want to share the entire contents of his brain? As far as he's concerned, there's no way his brilliance could be condensed into 200, 400, or even 4,000 words. Who cares about the audience's time constraints? They should stop whatever they're doing and pay attention to his pearls of wisdom.

If your success depends on getting your message across, you must throw off the shackles of excessive length and complexity, and say it simply.

Readability is your friend

The first step you need to take to achieve "short and sweet" is to get over yourself. Your audience doesn't care whether or not you went to college—and if you did—whether you attended an Ivy League university, graduated summa cum laude, got your Master's degree, or even your Ph.D. The fact that you read all of Proust in the French and Homer (the poet, not Mr. Simpson) in the Greek doesn't impress them one bit. Your vocabulary may be greater than William F. Buckley's and your library may be more extensive than that of Congress. They'll still be unmoved.

Leave your impressive education and credentials aside, and communicate at *no higher than* a 7th grade reading level.

Are we serious? Absolutely. We're going to show you that readability (the ease with which a document can be understood) is more than just a way to measure literacy—it's a guideline for creating communication that is simple, direct, and compelling.

Our role model: Toby Keith

There are lots of quotes from literary lions about simplicity (we'll probably throw in a couple before this chapter is done), but we think the person who says it best is country music singer Toby Keith, in a hit song called "A Little Less Talk and a Lot More Action." In the interest of brevity, we won't quote the entire lyric (written by Keith Hinton and Alan Stewart) but the title tells you everything you need to know: The hero (Toby Keith) finds he has a much more fulfilling (love) life by talking less, and acting more.

And, because audience members are all those things we've been describing throughout the book—busy, distracted, time-pressed, and cranky—they *want* a lower (i.e., simpler) reading level than ever before. *It's not that people don't know what words mean or can't comprehend complex sentence construction—it's that they don't want to.* Make life easy for them. If you do, they're more likely to pay attention.

A primer on readability and reading levels

If you want to have fun watching professors fight with each other, look up "readability" and "readability tests" (also called "reading level tests") in academic journals. Some experts swear by the idea that you can use a mathematical formula to test how understandable a sample of writing is, while others think it's a lot of bunk.

We believe that readability has value, if you use it as a screening guide—an early warning system—not an unbending rule to slavishly follow.

Here are some key facts you need to know:

1. Readability tests were first developed in the 1920s as a way to develop science textbooks that would be appropriate for different grade levels. The idea was to make sure the vocabulary and sentence structure of these books wouldn't be too difficult for the students who were learning biology or chemistry.
2. Most readability tests use mathematical equations to measure two elements of writing: the difficulty of words (semantics) and the difficulty of sentences (syntactics). (Yep, that's a real word.) They don't measure other aspects that affect reader ease, such as how ideas are organized or how the writing is formatted, nor do they test actual comprehension. Because readability tests were first created for school, the "score" is defined by grade level, instead of age or some other metric.

How communication rates

The average American reads at a 9th grade level. What that means, of course, is that the reading level does not necessarily correlate to educational background. Not all 7th graders can read a 7th grade text, and many college graduates are not able to read at a 12th grade level. On the whole though, reading ability is largely determined by a person's level of education and how extensively they read on an ongoing basis.

The bottom line about readability is this: To achieve a 7th grade reading level, you have to use simple words and short sentences. And to make your communication even more accessible, you need to make sure your tone is friendly, your structure is clear (see Chapter 7), and that the audience doesn't have to work to get through the communication or think too hard about what it means.

Reading level	Example
4th grade level	Comic strips, Ernest Hemingway's fiction
6th grade level	Popular fiction
7th grade level	Ads and marketing materials for consumer products
8th/9th grade level	*Reader's Digest*
10th grade level	*The New Yorker*

Is 7th grade *too* advanced?

Paul would argue that 6th grade, 5th grade, even 4th grade level is even better than 7th grade reading level. His position is that simpler is always better. It's no wonder he feels this way: This is the guy who emulates Hemingway (a high school graduate who wrote at a 4th grade level). But instead of debating the point, we recommend you analyze your audience to figure out the right level for what you're communicating.

We're not suggesting that you test everybody; that would understandably make them cranky. But you can make educated assumptions about how ready and able people are to read, based on demographics, including education and job levels. If you have a diverse audience, chances are good that reading levels are also diverse—which argues for making sure your materials are accessible to everyone.

Short. Simple. Sweet.

How do you improve your communication to make it more readable—more accessible and attractive? We have three suggestions, which are as easy as A, B, C:

A. *Keep it short.* Use short words, arranged in brief sentences, paragraphs, sections. (See page 145.)
B. *Make it simple.* Boil down your message to its essence. Illustrate and explain everything. (See Chapter 5.)
C. *Be sweet.* Use a friendly tone; be helpful and audience-focused. (See Chapter 3 and also refer back to Chapter 2 for more on meeting your audience's needs.)

Put your communication to the test

Two of the most widely used readability tests—the Flesch Reading Ease score, and the Flesch-Kincaid Grade Level score—are available on most versions of Microsoft Word, so you can evaluate your documents. Here's what you do:

1. Open your Microsoft Word document.
2. Under the "Tools" menu bar, click on "Spelling and Grammar."
3. At the bottom of the window that opens, click on the "Options" button.
4. Under the "Grammar" menu, check the box "Show Readability Statistics."
5. Now use the spelling/grammar checking feature as usual, accepting or rejecting Word's suggestions.
6. When Word is finished checking your document, a window will open that provides readability statistics.
7. To interpret the scores, click on the "Help" menu bar and search Word help for "readability."

A. Keep it short

You probably don't have time to read the newspaper on Saturday—we usually don't, either—but that means that on November 17, 2005, we both missed a great piece, "The need for speed," by staff writer Don Aucoin in *The Boston Globe*, about the trend toward extreme brevity, even when it comes to complex subjects.

Since you're so busy, we'll help you out by summing up the article: People have so little time to absorb information that almost every kind of communication—from books to broadcasts to sound bites—is getting shorter. (Stay tuned for a few examples.)

What it means, of course, is that if you're still creating long content, you have to stop. No one (except maybe the senior managers who review your work) has an Appétite for 3-screen e-mails, detailed Web pages, 1,500-word print articles, etc. You've simply got to condense and chop—or risk losing your audience altogether.

Mr. Aucoin cites a number of examples of how communication is slimming down. Here are 3 highlights:

- A British publisher recently issued *The 100-Minute Bible* that summarizes the Good Book into a 64-page paperback.
- In 2004, the average sound bite that network news shows allotted presidential candidates had shrunk to 8 seconds.
- Time-pressured Boston Red Sox fans can see a 2-hour compilation of each game—which still includes plenty of commercials—thanks to the regional cable network NESN, which broadcasts the condensed version at

midnight on game days. (According to the Elias Sports Bureau, in 2004, the average length of an American League game was 2:46:55 (2:47:20 in the National League), if you watch the games in real time. And that is down from about 3 hours on average, thanks to efforts by Major League Baseball to speed up the game (in the hopes of drawing more fans).

- Even the Oxford University Press has acknowledged that shorter might be better, by publishing a line of books on important events such as D-day, each of which has fewer than 100 pages.

The end of literacy as we know it? Nah, we think shorter is actually better. "You don't have to go on forever to be able to communicate important, fascinating, and complex ideas," says Leonard Steinhorn, a communications professor at American University in Washington, D.C. After all, maintains Mr. Steinhorn, one of the greatest speeches in history was the Gettysburg Address, which had only 272 words.

How to do short

✔ Narrow your focus to just one concept. (See Chapter 4.) Answer the question: What is the one thing I want my audience to know/do?

✔ Set strict guidelines for length—and stick to them. The average *USA Today* article is 300 words. Procter & Gamble, the big consumer products company, limits memos to 1 page. The best Web sites restrict items on the homepage to 100 words.

✔ Make your sentences direct and brief, and your paragraphs an easy-to-scan collection of just a few

18-year-olds, new media, and you

Here's yet another reason to keep it short. New forms of media are training people to receive information in shorter and shorter bursts. New media, of course, include the Internet, instant messaging, blogging, cell phones/picture phones, personal digital assistants (such as Palm and BlackBerry), MP3 players/iPods, satellite radio, TiVo/replay TV, and Web radio.

KEY RATES OF NEW MEDIA USAGE

New media usage	ages 18–24	ages 25–34	ages 35–54	ages 55+
Instant messaging	79.8%	68.3%	58.1%	43.1%
Text messaging	58.3%	46.1%	27.6%	8.3%
MP3/iPods	45.3%	29.9%	17.5%	6.7%
Web radio	44.4%	42.6%	33.0%	13.5%
Picture phones	30.6%	21.5%	14.6%	8.3%
Blogs	29.6%	21.7%	15.5%	11.1%

Source: BIGresearch, 2005

Not surprisingly, young people are the most avid users of new media. "The 18- to 24-year-olds have adopted new media more readily than any other age group," says Joe Pilotta, BIGresearch's vice president of research. "Not only do they use new media more, they are influenced by it much more . . . when it comes to making purchase decisions."

The key point: New media require that communication be very few words. Small screens and devices demand that you trim the fat and get right to the point—no wonder 18- to 24-year-olds have almost no tolerance for long content. That is unlikely to change as they get older—and people who are now 18 to 24 are going to be your audience for the next 50 years.

sentences. Remember: Sentences can consist of one word. (Ouch!) And paragraphs can consist of just one sentence.

✔ Choose short words. English is a gnarly language with a lot of words to choose from. "Altogether, about 200,000 English words are in common use, more than in German (184,000) and far more than in French (a mere 100,000)," writes Bill Bryson in *The Mother Tongue: English and How It Got That Way.*

Our language is also a mixed bag: Because of the way England was occupied early in its history by Romans, Anglo-Saxons, Scandinavians, and Normans, English words come from a variety of roots.

But the simplest words in English stem from the Anglo-Saxons—those simple, direct, no-nonsense people. Mr. Bryson writes that the words that survive from Anglo-Saxon "are among the most fundamental words in English: man, wife, child, brother, sister, live, fight, love, drink, sleep, eat, horse and so on."

(Note that they're also short words.)

Today, half the words in almost any sample of writing (with the exception of corporate announcements and legal documents) are of Anglo-Saxon origin and every one of the 100 most common words in English is Anglo-Saxon.

"To this day, we have an almost instinctive preference for the older Anglo-Saxon phrases," Mr. Bryson writes, because those words are short and direct.

When all else fails: Edit your work

It's odd for writers (who love the flow of their own prose a little too much) to give the following advice, but we feel obligated to do so (especially since we follow it): After you are completely satisfied with what you've written, cut it. Dramatically.

> *If I had more time, I would have written you a shorter letter.—Mark Twain*

Twain was right, of course. The key to improving what you have written—not only making it shorter, but also more interesting, more informative and, heck, more entertaining—is taking the time to do it.

(Please don't) "increase your word power"

For 60 years, *Reader's Digest* **has published** a popular column called "Increase Your Word Power," which invites readers to enhance their vocabulary by taking a multiple-choice word definition self-test. The premise, of course, is that the more words you know, the better off—more confident, capable, and sophisticated—you'll be.

"Increase Your Word Power" is so successful that that monthly column has spawned such line extensions as books, an online game, and even a spelling-bee type national contest for students. There's nothing wrong with this (who wants to denigrate/disparage/degrade/belittle/malign/defame personal development?) except when it comes to grabbing the attention of your audience. You know all the words you need. Resist the temptation to use long words to sound educated or erudite (there goes one of those words now)—just say what you mean, as plainly as possible.

Your audience will thank you for it.

Painful as it is, you have to be your own editor, even if you have someone else reviewing your stuff. The reason? The best person to improve what you have created is you. But the only way to improve is to invest the time to do it. Here are 2 ways:

1. *After you think you are done, go for a walk.*
   Get a cup of coffee. If time is tight, just stare out the window for a couple of minutes and think of anything other than what you have just written. You want to clear your mind as much as possible. That way when you return—whether that is in 10 minutes or the next day—to what you have written, you will be able to find places to cut fairly easily. ("What was I thinking when I wrote that?")
   "Wasting time" leads to better writing.

2. *Start at the top.*
   Okay, you have read the thing over once and have made some cuts. Now look at what you have written a second time. Start with the lead. Does it make people want to read on; is it as good as it possibly could be? Let's go back to how we began this section. We could have written:

   Mark Twain knew something about writing. Almost 150 years after he gave us Huck, Tom, and Becky, stories about raftin' down rivers, and Connecticut Yankees in King Arthur's court, the words of the man born Samuel L. Clemens live on. So we probably want to pay attention to the few writing tips he left behind. Perhaps the best known wasn't presented as a tip but as an aside in a note he sent to a friend.

"The wastebasket is a writer's best friend."

Isaac Bashevis Singer,
Nobel-prize winning author

Would that first paragraph have worked? Sure.

But it would not have been as good as what we began with. The Twain quote that begins the section is only 13 words, so we get off to a faster start. Plus quoting him in the lead has the advantage of using one of the world's best writers to make the key point about what this section is all about.

The moral: Always see if you can get off to a better start.

B. Make it simple

If Simple were a person, she'd be the younger sister of Short. They'd be very close, doing almost everything together. They'd like the same music (pop songs under 2 minutes long), movies (action films with lots of quick cuts and not too much dialogue), and men (thin, metrosexual types who buy their clothes at the Gap).

But Simple (the person) would be more focused on helping people than Short. Simple's the type to explain things clearly, even if it means taking a little more time or space. She'd make a great elementary school teacher or tour guide. She'd never want anyone to be confused or left behind.

Like its namesake, simple (the concept) is all about service. The premise is—you guessed it—simple.

As Alison's client Kevin Kelly puts it, "Never underestimate anyone's intelligence or overestimate their knowledge." We start with the premise that the audience is smart, but we don't assume they know exactly where Paraguay is located, or the difference between a plasma and an LCD television, or what LCD stands for, anyway. Along the same lines, it's

Simple inspiration: *Real Simple*

If you're looking for a role model on how to be simple, look no further than the latest issue of *Real Simple* magazine.

Founded in 2000, the publication's mission is to "give women the information, inspiration, and tools they can use to enjoy easier, more balanced lives. . . . We help our readers do what they need to do, so they have more time to enjoy what they want to do."

Real Simple features beautiful visuals, spare copy, and a clean layout. And the content is all about fulfilling its mission to help the audience. Here's a sampling of articles from the May 2005 issue:

- 3-step cleaning guide: easy solutions for difficult tasks
- Clear mental clutter (and get more done)
- Quick workout upgrades: small changes, big results

somebody's first day—at work, at school, or in town—today. The old-timers may have a deep base of knowledge about "the way things work around here," but somebody in your audience doesn't have a clue what something means, or even where to find out. It's your job to explain it to them.

Even the most experienced and knowledgeable people forget sometimes—or maybe they just missed the meeting where the topic was covered. And if you think you're supposed to know something that everyone else seems to know, you're too embarrassed to ask a question. So you spend the rest of your life not knowing what they mean when they use a certain acronym, like, say, LCD.

How to do simple

✔ *Choose words and terms that are familiar to the largest percentage of your audience.* If you use any word or term where there's even the slightest possibility that it might be unfamiliar, define it. Don't worry about insulting the people who know what the term means—if you routinely use definitions, the audience will see that it's just the helpful way you do things.

✔ *Avoid jargon, technical, or scientific language or "corporate speak"* (that stiff, lawyer-sounding, big-word-laden

Mr. Simplicity makes his case

We go to a lot of conferences, where we listen to a lot of speakers. And it's rare that you remember what a speaker talked about the next day, much less years later.

But Mike Rawlings, president of Pizza Hut from 1997 to 2003, who is credited with turning the company around, made an impact on us. At a conference, Mr. Rawlings spoke about his theories of leadership and communication, which all center on simplicity.

Here are just a few of Mr. Rawlings's words of wisdom:

- "Why should we simplify? People are busy, and they appreciate the effort you make. By simplifying, you honor those people."
- "Simplifying takes a tremendous amount of thought. It requires a lot more effort."
- "Complexity is terrific screen for the false. If you don't understand, it's tough to tell what rings true."
- "CEOs are not simplifiers. They have gotten to where they are today by handling complex issues. As a result, they are not interested in the zen of business leadership. This is a problem because employees need simplicity to understand clearly what they should do."

nonsense you find in annual reports). If someone insists that you use this junk, move it way down in your content, after you've included clear headlines, a nice short summary, breakheads, sidebars, and other chunked content. (See Chapter 7 for more on how to do this.)

✓ *Identify people, places, and things.* Tell us that Bill Bryson (the author we quoted earlier) is best known for his travel narratives, *A Walk in the Woods* and *In a Sunburned Country* (oops, we forgot to do this), that Springfield, where the Simpsons live, is a city in Illinois (maybe) and that LCD stands for "liquid crystal display," a type of screen used for televisions and computer monitors (finally, we told you).

C. Be sweet

Bet you're wondering what we mean by "sweet." Are we obsessed with Milky Way bars and rocky road ice cream?

Actually, yes, but in this case we're referring not to "sweet" as in "pleasing to the taste," but to the second set of meanings of the word (which, by the way, is of Anglo-Saxon origin). From Webster's *Ninth New Collegiate Dictionary*:

2a. pleasing to the mind and feelings
2b. marked by gentle good humor kindliness

Being short and simple is not enough to be appealing to your audience: The third essential element is to communicate in a friendly tone. An authentic voice. An approach that is clearly person-to-person, not Monolithic Corporate Entity to Lowly Individual.

Unfortunately, we spend so much time these days feeling like a tiny cog in the wheel, lost in a high-tech maze, reduced to nothing more than a number and a password. So we crave the human touch. We love walking into the local hardware store and knowing the shopkeeper, who gives us advice not based on guiding us to the most expensive solution, but what's best for us. ("This 45-cent bolt should do the trick.")

We bring that person-to-person preference to communication as well. (After all, we'd much rather receive a personal letter than an anonymous mass mailing.) But even if we're receiving something from someone we don't know, we'd like to feel that there's a person behind the communication (who, by the way, cares about us and wants to help us).

The personality of communication is often called "voice." Every communication has a voice—from the bureaucratic tone of government reports to the fun, energetic style of Target ads.

The best way to engage your audience is to uncover your authentic voice and let your wonderful personality come through. That's how you achieve "sweet" (pleasing to the mind and feelings)—by putting yourself into your communication so that your audience can recognize and relate to you.

All about you—no, we mean the real you

Throughout this book, we've gently suggested (okay, strongly urged) that the way to get your audience's attention is to make communication about their needs and interests. But here's where you—the person creating the communication—come in.

The voice of doom

We're advocating that you use your real voice to making your communication feel compelling and authentic. To inspire you, we invited you to look at these negative role models, where the voice is stiff, bureaucratic, and close to inhuman:

- **U.S. government agencies.** Those Department of Labor or Department of Defense reports, for example. Don't you feel the dust of bureaucracy invading your lungs? (Interestingly enough, the government-created consumer-oriented materials are quite helpful and friendly. We guess they let those people out of the basement.)
- **Academic journals.** Who first decided that they should be written in such a stilted way? It's like a secret code language, just for old guys in silly gowns.
- **High school textbooks.** The guaranteed way to turn off a 15-year-old is to talk down to him. At length. And yet textbooks do it. Makes you wonder if the authors ever met a teenager. Or if they ever were teenagers themselves.

Your audience wants to hear from you, not from the department or company you work for. This is not the time to hide your light behind your cubicle walls; you need to let the real you—complete with bad jokes, an exhaustive knowledge of Civil War history, and a collection of every CD Bruce Springsteen even sneezed on—come through.

This may be a little scary because it means you can't disguise yourself (You know what Bruce sang: "Is that you, baby, or just a brilliant disguise?") or hide behind your public identities: Mr. MBA. Ms. Director of Training. Mr. VP of Logistics.

No, it should be the real you, creating communication only for the person you're trying to reach. Just the 2 of you, alone on the porch swing on a summer's evening. The stars in the sky and the cicadas humming. Feels kind of nice, doesn't it?

How to do sweet

✔ **Write like you talk.** Many of us get a pen or a keyboard in our hands, and we stiffen up as if we're on our best behavior in school. We want to sound impressive, so we become more formal. If this happens to you, try 2 things: First, read your work out loud to make sure it sounds conversational and real. Second, if you still have trouble being conversational, record what you want to say on a tape recorder, then use the recording as the basis for your communication.

✔ **If you're creating communication as part of a group, for a larger organization, work with other communicators to agree on the "voice" of your organization.** In the words of Steve Peha, partner in the Word Factory, a company that teaches writing: "Ask yourselves, 'If our company were a person, who would that person be? Is the organization friendly or more formal? What unique

What to do differently

✔ Be as brief as possible. Ask yourself, "Could I say this even more directly, with fewer words?"

✔ Help your audience understand the content. Make things simple. Explain and define what they might not instantly understand.

✔ Be yourself. The audience doesn't want an impersonal communication; they want to feel like they're hearing from a living, breathing, imperfect human being.

characteristics make our organization distinctive?' Never forget that you're a real person communicating with other people. Even if you're creating communication for a large organization, preserve that one-to-one feeling."

Finding and defining your organization's "voice" may seem abstract but you don't have to look far to see organizations that do it successfully:

- IBM is smart and knowledgeable.
- Virgin is adventurous and creative.
- Apple is innovative and stylish.

➡ INSIGHT 9:
The unvarnished truth
about reading levels

As you can tell by this chapter, we've been thinking a lot lately about reading levels. Our conclusion is that most communication is written at too high a level. You need to make your communication simpler, not because audience members are illiterate (although illiteracy does exist); but because your audience is busy, distracted, and reluctant to read complicated prose.

In the interest of exploring the issue further, Alison decided to do some research and started wandering around the Internet, seeing what educators and others had to say about reading levels. In the course of her travels, she came across a Web site (*www.brainchild.com*) that allows visitors to take a free reading test based on state standards for competency in reading and math.

A few clicks of the mouse later and Alison (who is from New Jersey) was taking her state's 7th grade reading test.

" Be sincere, be brief, be seated. **"**

President Franklin D. Roosevelt on speechmaking

The test consisted of two passages—one about a place in North Carolina called Blowing Rock and the other about the blizzard of 1888—each followed by 6 multiple choice questions. Piece of cake, right? Alison skimmed through the passages, clicked on the answers, and waited for her score.

Which was (drum roll, please): 67 percent. That's right, boys and girls, Ms. English major (with high honors no less), avid reader, terrific speller barely passed the test.

Naturally, Alison's reaction was, "There must be some mistake." Nope. She checked: She got 3 questions wrong, and forgot to answer another one. Because of the way the test was weighted, 67 percent was indeed her embarrassing grade.

Then she began making excuses. "Well, I did the whole thing in under 5 minutes," Alison said to herself. And: "I got interrupted in the middle." And: "I don't care about these topics, anyway, so it's no wonder I didn't really pay attention."

And then the light dawned. The way Alison read those boring passages—and dealt with the questions on the test—was exactly the way most audience members read the stuff we send them. Sometimes they're a little interested in the topic; other times, they're merely indifferent. But they're always thinking about other things, skimming to find the most relevant parts, skipping other sections, and getting interrupted in the middle.

In fact, when you think about, maybe 67 percent is not such a bad score. After all, if your audience retained two-thirds of the message you sent them, you'd feel as if you'd accomplished something, right?

Despite this self-justification, Alison was feeling a little depressed. So she decided to take a detour from comprehension and visit a very different type of Web site: *www.cs.utexas.edu/users/jbc/home/chef.html.*

This valuable and unique tool helps you translate your messages into four completely useless but hysterical dialects: Jive. Pig Latin. Valley girl. And Swedish Chef (that famous Muppet character).

It's really easy to do. You simply take a passage of writing, put it into the text box, and choose the language you want to translate it into.

For example, let's say you've just received senior management's first draft on the company's new direction:

> *Our new strategy will center on providing distinctive, consumer-oriented products and services to members in targeted markets. By focusing more sharply on the customer segments that align with our strengths and offer the best profit potential, we will be better able to provide consumers with a wider range of product choices, including more open access products. And we can add value by providing customers with information that helps them improve the quality of health care.*

Pretty dry and corporate, isn't it? You're worried that, like other high-level messages you're forced to deal with, it will be sent to the audience and then disappear into the ether, without making the slightest impression on anyone.

You need to inject some life into this writing. Maybe it would be more compelling in jive? Let's give an excerpt a try (see following page).

Our new strategy gots'ta centa' on providin' dis-
tinctive, consumer-o'iented products and services
t'members in targeted markets. By focusin' mo'e
sharply on de customa' segments dat align wid
our strengds and offa' de best profit potential,
we gots'ta be betta' able t'provide consumers wid
some wida' range uh product choices, includin'
mo'e jimmey access products. What it is, Mama!

Much, much better. Would it be even more effective in Swedish Chef? Let's give that first sentence a whirl:

Ooor noo stretegy veell center oon prufeeding
deestinctife-a, cunsoomer-ooreeented prudoocts
und serfeeces tu members in tergeted merkets.

Hmm, maybe not. And although Pig Latin has some appeal—after all, don't a lot of corporate messages seem like they're written to obscure instead of explain?—and valley girl is tempting, you, like, feel that jive almost had the exact tone you sought, you know? But, it wasn't, like, really you.

So, go ahead. Visit the Web page. Do the translation. Hit the send button. It may not improve your readability, but at least you'll have something to chuckle about in the unemployment line.

10 | Write a recipe

"Don't do that."
"Do as I say."
"Just do it."

THESE COMMANDS CERTAINLY catch our attention, but there's also something about them that makes us adults want to throw ourselves on the floor, kicking and screaming, "Just say no!"

We don't want to be treated like children anymore. We haven't struggled through all those years of school, work, and the annoyances that come with day-to-day adult reality to be lectured to. We never liked to be ordered around, and our tolerance has declined as we've gotten older. In fact, as you read in Chapter 9, this resistance to rules is so strong that we bristle even when the tone of a communication reminds us of commands.

Recipes, not rules

But, although we rail against rules, the interesting thing about human beings is that we don't mind instructions, guidelines, and (with the exception of guys who are lost while driving) directions. We're happy to accept guidance if it helps us accomplish something that matters.

That's why "how to" is such a powerful phrase. And it's why a key way to get your audience's attention is to provide

In a world filled with rules, your audience doesn't need more procedures, regulations, and admonitions. What people want most is a friendly helping hand to help them solve problems and get stuff done. If you provide that, you're sure to get and keep your audience's attention.

a "recipe": helpful advice that makes at least one aspect of their lives easier. Note the difference:

✓ A rule tells you something you must do, stated as a command. The body language that accompanies a rule is a wagging finger pointed at the offender.

✓ A recipe helps you do something you *want* to do, expressed as a set of suggestions. The accompanying body language is a hand on your shoulder, offering encouragement.

Move people in your direction

Marketing communication expert Jonathan Kranz, author of *Writing Copy for Dummies*, offer this perspective on the value of recipes. According to Mr. Kranz, collateral—brochures and other printed sales material used to promote a company and its products or services—often falls short, because it focuses on "me" (as in, "Here's why I'm so wonderful.") instead of "you" (as in, "How can I help you?").

When creating marketing materials, instead of listing every positive attribute about yourself, your company, and what you're selling, Mr. Kranz recommends reversing the focus: *Answer the prospective buyer's need*. Specifically, Mr. Kranz advises identifying what prospects do between their initial interest and making a purchase, and providing information to respond to that process.

"Do prospects conduct research? Share information with others? Require specifications? Daydream about the successful resolution of their challenge?

"Once you understand what prospects do to make a decision, you can provide useful material that meets their needs and therefore motivates them to buy," says Mr. Kranz.

Answer the prospective buyer's need. ▶▶

Too many rules

Since anything that resembles a rule is such a turn-off, it's surprising that so much of communication today has its origin in rules. Consider a sampling you may have seen recently:

- An e-mail from the division president describing the new procedures you have to follow when you travel on business.
- A letter from your health insurance company warning you about benefits changes.
- Instructions on a Web site, listing an array of caveats and clauses, explaining the company's refund policy.
- A voice mail message from your mother nagging you to call your brother for his birthday.

Chances are that material isn't a traditional brochure, but something more helpful—something much more like a recipe.

The crucial ingredient in all these materials is help; the purpose is not to "hard sell" the prospect, but to provide information that helps the prospect answer a concern or solve a problem.

Hints from Heloise

There are many places you can go for inspiration on how to be helpful: Turn on the television and watch HGTV (Home and Garden Television), pick up a consumer magazine like *Cooking Light*, browse the craft section at your local bookstore, or listen to "Car Talk" on National Public Radio. But our favorite, which is one of the longest-running, can be found in a newspaper near you: the column called "Hints from Heloise."

It all started in 1959 when a Honolulu housewife named Heloise Cruse decided she wanted to write a newspaper column to help other housewives do their chores more effectively. So she approached the editor of the *Honolulu Advertiser* about her idea, offering to work for free for 30 days as a trial. Her column, "The Reader's Exchange," was such a success that in 1961 *Time* magazine reported on it, and soon the column, renamed "Hints from Heloise," became syndicated to newspapers around the world.

Today's "Heloise" is Ms. Cruse's daughter Poncé, who took over the column when her mother died in 1977.

Heloise's ongoing success is simple to understand: In her newspaper column (which runs 7 days a week in 500 newspapers), her monthly *Good Housekeeping* column, her books, and her radio and TV appearances, Heloise offers simple, clear advice on a wide array of practical problems. The tone is helpful and matter-of-fact. When Heloise

Material that motivates

How-to information that supports a prospect's decision-making process, according to Mr. Kranz, can take a number of forms, including:

- White papers (reports that offer research and analysis on relevant issues)
- Magazines or newspapers (that you produce)
- Guides
- Case studies
- How-to instructions
- Specification sheets

"It is good to obey all the rules when you're young, so you'll have the strength to break them when you're old."

Mark Twain

answers a reader question, she takes the concern (no matter how trivial) very seriously.

And in imparting advice, she never lectures—she just provides recipes for daily living in a chatty conversational tone.

For instance, here's an excerpt from the November 30, 2005, column:

> **Don't you love coming up with other ways to use everyday items in the home? For instance, inexpensive paper plates (cheap, white ones) have many great uses in the kitchen and all around the house. Here are just a few to get you thinking:**
>
> - **They are great as an instant dish cover in the microwave to keep flood splatters contained, or under the dish for easy cleanup if something boils over.**
> - **For a quick dustpan, cut one in half to scoop up spills or to remove swept-up dust.**

Heloise even uses advice to make a sales pitch. One page on her Web site (*Heloise.com*, of course) features her books, with a cover photo and a short description of each edition, along with a link to *Amazon.com* (so you can buy right now). But Heloise doesn't stop there; she includes "hints" on how to buy:

> - **If you are going to a bookstore to purchase my book, call first to be sure they have it in stock, so you don't waste a trip.**

- *Visit my Web site often to check out events, local TV, and radio shows I'll be doing in your city. Whenever I'm on a book tour, I always try to stop by every book store I can to sign copies of my book, so even if I haven't done an official book signing in your city, you might find an autographed copy!*
- *If you send me a self-addressed, stamped envelope with your request, I'll be happy to sign book plates that you can put in the book— especially if you're picking up several as gifts.*

Subtle, helpful—and brilliant! We're stealing this idea for our Web site. (See how we've done so on our Web site *www.yourattentionpleasebook.com*.)

3 ways to write recipes

How can you provide your audience with helpful advice that will get their attention? We'll describe 3 ways:

1. Tips (see below)
2. Instructions (see page 172)
3. Recipes (see page 177)

1. Terrific tips

The simplest approach to offering how-to information is the "tip," a small helpful bit of advice that prospects can skim quickly.

Tips are popular because they are easy to create—you are communicating what you know in bite-sized bits—and just as easy for the audience to digest.

Here are 5 key tips on creating tips:

✓ **Keep them short.**

✓ **Make them simple.** Tips are not the right venue for explaining complex topics or taking the audience through every step of a procedure. (Use instructions or recipes when creating involved how-tos.)

✓ **Use active verbs** (such as "keep," "make," "write," and "use"). Verbs always signify action, and tips are all about action.

✓ **Use bullets** when tips don't require a particular sequence. (Actually, we like checkmarks instead of bullets because they suggest a to-do list) and a numbered list (1, 2, 3, 4 . . .) when the tips should be followed in order.

✓ **Understand the limitations of tips.** Once you get the hang of tips, it's tempting to use them *everywhere*. But, as with almost anything, it's possible to go too far. Too many tips become exhausting—like a to-do list that just won't quit. So, here's a tip: Do use tips, just do so judiciously.

2. Clear instructions

While tips are like tapas—small, appetizer-sized morsels that the Spanish combine to make a light meal (with wine)—instructions are a full meal, potatoes, and a side vegetable. They're a sit-down dinner: Filling and nourishing, instructions provide detailed directions that get people ready to jump up (after asking to be excused from the table), ready to take action.

According to Richard Saul Wurman, the information expert we first quoted in Chapter 1, "Half of all our communication is the giving and receiving of instructions."

Smart tips for communicators

As we mentioned before, Alison's firm produces an electronic newsletter called *Smart Tips* that has proven to be an effective way to promote her company. E-mailed to clients and prospects every other Monday, *Smart Tips* is designed to provide simple, practical information on how to improve employee communication that readers can absorb in less than 10 minutes. (Issues are also archived on Alison's company Web site, *www.davisandco.com.* Just click on "resources.")

By any measure—feedback from subscribers, "opens" (the percentage of people who click on the issue to read it), and "click throughs" (the number of people who click on related links or forward the newsletter to others)—we have found that *Smart Tips* is successful at grabbing and holding its audience's attention.

"*Smart Tips* gives me information I can use to do my job better," wrote one subscriber recently. "That makes it worth my while."

That may be the best definition we have ever heard of how you know whether a "tip" has been effective.

Here's an excerpt from a recent issue on how to make employee newsletters and other print publications more effective. You can see how *Smart Tips* is all about tips:

- **Make publications service-oriented.** Write from the employee's viewpoint, making it your mission to help employees understand key issues so they can see where they fit and know how to make a contribution.

- **Leverage visuals.** Follow best practices of external magazines to tell your stories through photographs, charts, graphs, and other lively visuals.

- **Give your audience the choice of skimming or reading.** Depending upon their interest in the topic, some people will just scan—looking quickly at the headline, subheads, photo captions, and sidebars—while others will devour every word. Make sure your content is chunked out to appeal to both casual skimmers and avid readers.

"Are you ready to order?"

Instructions happen all the time in everyday life—in fact, they're so commonplace, we often don't even identify them as instructions. Mr. Wurman cites the simple act of ordering a meal in a restaurant as a sequence of instructions: "We give instructions to the waiter. The waiter recodes what we've said in his own or her own way, and takes this group of instructions in a different format, written instead of verbal, into the kitchen, and then gives instructions to a series of people in the kitchen to produce something."

Since so much of communication is instructions, they should be easy, right? Actually, no, as anyone who's ever tried to learn to knit, assemble a piece of Swedish furniture, or fill out a tax return can attest.

The fault in almost every case? The person giving instructions assumes knowledge the person following the instructions just doesn't have. (The folks at the IRS who describe how to fill out form 1040—the standard tax return—know what "adjusted gross income" means, but most mere mortals don't.)

Effective instructions need to be developed without a single assumption about the audience's knowledge or ability.

Yes, our audience is smart, but we must pretend that they've just been beamed onto the planet and have never seen a knitting needle or an Allen wrench or an IRS agent who can explain exactly what adjusted gross income means. (We know. You're dying to learn the definition. So, here goes a simplified definition: Adjusted gross income is what you and I would call income—wages—plus some stuff you might or might not consider income—interest and capital gains—plus stuff you wouldn't think of as income but is—income from retirement accounts and alimony paid to you—adjusted downward by specific deductions—such as contributions to deductible retirement accounts, and alimony paid *by* you—but *not* by including standard and itemized deductions.) [We really must get a life.]

AGI is the number you write at the bottom of page 1 of your 1040 form, and then, because bureaucrats believe in redundancy, copy again to the top of page 2.

The best instructions start from scratch, like a completely empty page, and illustrate and explain absolutely everything.

Luckily, Mr. Wurman in his 1991 book *Follow the Yellow Brick Road: Learning to Give, Take, and Use Instructions* provides great instructions for creating instructions.

His formula is simple and effective. All instructions should have the following 6 components:

Mission. The purpose or aim of the instruction.

Destination. The end result.

Procedure. The specific directions.

Time. Amount of time it will take to complete the process.

Anticipation. Things you should expect along the way.

Failure. How to know if something went wrong.

Come to our holiday open house!

The easiest way to illustrate this process is with driving directions, one of the most common instructions in life, and one of the most fraught with peril. (Hello, MapQuest, are you listening?)

Here's how Mr. Wurman's formula plays out in directions inviting someone to a holiday party at your house:

Mission	Please come to our party.
Destination	At our house on December 17 at 6 P.M.
Procedure	Take the Garden State Parkway north or south to Exit 131. At the end of the ramp, at the traffic light, make a left onto Pleasant Valley Way. Take Pleasant Valley Way for 4.5 miles, passing 3 traffic lights, to Midland Avenue, which is the 4th traffic light. Make a left at Midland Avenue, and continue for 2 miles (Midland turns into Elm Street) past 1 traffic light to our house, 123 Elm Street.
Time	From midtown Manhattan it will take about an hour, depending on traffic. It is 40 miles from Times Square.
Anticipation	Our house is a white Victorian farmhouse with light green shutters and a white picket fence out front. (You will probably hear the world's most obnoxious dog barking. He is harmless. Big and bouncy, but harmless.)
Failure	If you get to the light at Prospect Street, you've gone too far.

"The same building blocks can be used to compose wildly diverse instructions," writes Mr. Wurman, including "telling someone to fly a kite, program a VCR, or develop a business plan."

How specific?

With instructions, being very specific is desirable, but there's a line you don't want to cross, where instructions become rules. As Mr. Wurman warns, "The chances for clarity increase as a message becomes absolute. The search for the perfect instruction content requires finding the balance between clarity and constraint, between the relative and the absolute. There is magic in the ambiguity of the relative, but there is also confounding mystery."

3. Precise recipes

Many information experts (including Richard Saul Wurman) would not make the distinction between instructions and recipes, but we suspect those experts have never sweated over a soufflé that failed to rise in the kitchen while the new in-laws are waiting in the dining room. While instructions

How to use instructions

Instructions have a wide array of applications to business and other communication. Here are just a few ways to use instructions to give your communication more audience appeal:

✓ What to do to order something, especially if you want to encourage ordering in large quantities or quick ordering. Amazon.com is the best role model for easy-to-follow ordering instructions.

✓ How to follow a process, such as enrolling in medical benefits or completing a time card or requesting a purchase order.

✓ To manage exceptions. Often people understand the usual way to do things, but they need help with the unusual. Make sure you give step-by-step instructions with every situation.

need to be clear, recipes (whether for cooking, chemistry, or computers) need the highest degree of precision.

That's why, even if you never intend to invent a new lemon meringue pie, it's helpful to understand how to write a recipe. If you train yourself to be as precise as is required to create a recipe, all your communication will be clearer and easier to understand.

Recipes 101

How to write a recipe? Let's ask those paragons of precision, the Brits, or more specifically, the British Nutrition Foundation, a scientific and educational charity, which

The origin of recipes

Cooking throughout the ages has mostly involved oral history—your grandmother makes something, she shows your mother, who then shows you, and nothing ever needs to be written down. But recipes emerged when more rigor was needed.

Israeli food and wine writer Daniel Rogov believes that recipes were first used during the sixth century B.C. when the Persian leader Cyrus the Great decreed that everyone in the army needed to fight.

"Not even the cooks of generals were exempt," writes Mr. Rogov on his Web site, *www .stratsplace.com/rogov,* and that meant that from day to day even the best of cooks might die in battle and his recipes, all of which were stored in his head, would be lost.

"The generals were not as concerned about the death of their cooks as they were about the fact that their favorite dishes could no longer be served. The practice thus began of using captured soldiers and other hostages to formally record the recipes of whatever cook happened to be alive on any given day."

"promotes the well being of society through the impartial interpretation and effective dissemination of evidence-based nutritional knowledge and advice." (They sound like they know what they're doing, don't they? And the best part is, you just have to follow the guidelines, you don't actually have to eat British food. That is a good thing because there is a reason that in the history of mankind, no one has ever said, "I feel like going out to eat tonight and having "British.")

The foundation recommends that every recipe be made up of 3 parts:

1. A list of all the ingredients needed
2. A list of all the equipment
3. The method—how to make the dish

And since the British Nutrition Foundation deals with schools and other organizations with members who may not know much at all about cooking, the "method" tends to be very basic.

For example, what if the recipe you're making calls for a chopped onion, and you've never chopped an onion before. As you can see by the directions below, the Brits will explain it all to you.

How to chop an onion
1. Cut away the top of the onion.
2. Peel away the outer brown skin.
3. Cut the onion in half.
4. Slice lengthways, ensuring that you do not cut all the way.
5. Slice across the onion.

Lime in the coconut

When your workday is done, you still need recipes, as Dennis G. Jerz, associate professor of English in the department of new media journalism at Seton Hall University, will attest. Mr. Jerz, who writes extensively about how to communicate clearly using electronic "new media," offers this example of how to write a recipe simply and clearly (*see box below*).

Making a lime and coconut drink

These instructions describe how to make one serving of the beverage described in the "Lime in the Coconut" song. It also explains what to do if the drink makes you sick, and suggests ways you might try to get the annoying tune out of your head.

I. Preparing the drink

You will need one (1) lime and one (1) coconut.

1. Take lime.
2. Take coconut.
3. Put the lime in the coconut.
4. Drink it right up.

II. If you get sick

Drinking the lime and the coconut may result in indigestion. In case of a bellyache, do the following:

1. Call the doctor.
2. Wake him up (if necessary).
3. Say, "Doctor! Is there nothing I can take, I say Doctor! To relieve this belly ache!"

III. Suggestions for getting the tune out of your head

You might try any or all of the following. Repeat as necessary, until the ringing in your ears drowns out the song, or until you lose consciousness.

- Hit yourself on the head with the coconut, or
- Listen to a Britney Spears album

⮕ INSIGHT 10:
Julie's perfect apple pie

Alison learned to cook as a teenager (which is a lot of years ago), and she's always enjoyed it, so today she is a comfortable, capable cook who can use recipes, adapt them, ignore them, or make up stuff as she goes along. ("Let's see: I've got chicken, dried apricots, bacon, and sherry. I can whip up dinner with those ingredients.")

But recently Alison had an epiphany that helped her understand the importance of recipes. Alison's colleague Julie, who's brand-new to cooking, needed to make her first apple pie. And to increase the degree of difficulty, the pie had to be perfect: It was the featured dessert for Thanksgiving dinner. Julie was being asked to fill in as pie baker for her sister who was away at veterinary school, and whose apple pie was legendary. And the family and friends who would be at the dinner were all very good cooks and very particular about the quality of their food. (No canned yams or Pillsbury prepared rolls would be served at this dinner!)

Naturally, Julie was a little apprehensive (well, panicked, actually). And although several friends advised her to take the easy way out and buy a pie, Julie was determined to rise to the occasion and make the pie completely from scratch.

The key to her success, Julie decided, would be a really good recipe. Experienced cooks like Alison were almost no help because they had been making apple pie for so long they didn't even use a recipe: "Just peel and cut up some apples, sprinkle sugar and cinnamon, cover with crumb crust and bake until it's done." Julie needed extremely specific directions. The seat of someone's pants was just not helpful.

Luckily, we are living in an Internet world, and Julie is an Internet girl. She searched the Web like nobody's business, spending the most time on a terrific site called *www.epicurious.com*, which features recipes from leading cooking magazines, including *Bon Appétit* and *Gourmet*. Typing "apple pie" in the Epicurious search box brings up 42 recipes, and Julie examined every blessed one of them.

"First, I eliminated the funky ones that seemed to have odd ingredients, like cranberries, because I wanted to make a traditional apple pie," Julie recalls. "And then I narrowed down the choices based on how specific the recipe seemed to be. I didn't want to leave anything to chance or have to use my own judgment."

On Thanksgiving eve, she settled on "Cinnamon Crumble Apple Pie" from the October 2003 issue of *Bon Appétit* because it met her criteria for precision—and she loves crumbs.

What to do differently

✓ Provide your audience with how-to information that will help them do their jobs better or make their lives easier.

✓ Use tips when the information you want to convey is short, simple, and bite-sized.

✓ Create instructions when you need to be more specific about what people should do.

✓ Write recipes when the greatest level of precision is required.

"What I liked about the recipe was that both the ingredient list and the preparation instructions were divided into 3 categories: crust, filling, and topping," said Julie. "Everything followed along in sequence. It was all very explicit."

How did Julie do? There were a few anxious moments: How much flour should she use to roll out the crust? The recipe called for a food processor—was it okay that she didn't have one? When rolling out the dough, what should she do if it breaks? As a result, there were a couple of early Thanksgiving morning phone calls to her vet school sister.

But, in general, Julie felt that the recipe served her well. "When I started to mix the crumbs together, I got nervous because they didn't resemble crumbs that I had seen on pies. But there in the recipe was the reassurance: 'Cut in until mixture resembles wet sand.' That made me feel that I was on the right track."

Everything took a long time, but a couple of hours after she started preparations, Julie took the pie out of the oven. It was beautiful! She carefully carried it to the dinner, where the host displayed it in a place of honor among the other desserts.

And when the turkey had been consumed and the desserts were served, everyone agreed: Julie's pie was delicious. In fact, it was perfect.

Section 4: Putting These Ideas into Practice

11 | Learn by example

A different way to review what we have covered in the book

All too often, communication makes a misstep and loses its way, and, in doing so, loses the attention of the audience. In this chapter, we'll sum up the advice we've given throughout the book by telling you what *not* to do.

AT FIRST, we were going to call this chapter, "When Bad Things Happen to Good Communicators."

Or we were going to take a page from the popular Condé Nast young women's magazine *Glamour* and give you a list of "*Glamour* Don'ts." (For those of you not familiar with the monthly feature, it shows photographs of women making dreadful fashion mistakes, with their identities disguised by black tape over their eyes.)

Or we were going to call this section, "Please don't try this at home (or in the office)."

Whatever name we decided to give Chapter 11, the intent would have been the same: to continue to steer you in the direction of grabbing your audience's attention. Throughout this book, we've tried a variety of methods to illustrate our advice, and now we're going to sum it all up by emphasizing what *not* to do.

So here goes: The bad and the ugly, organized as "The 7 Deadly Sins of Poor Communication." To help you tie the content back in to the main points of the book, we've included references to relevant chapters.

Sin 1: Making it all about "me"

A well-known health care company whose name we won't mention has a monthly employee newsletter that's filled with content the CEO wants to communicate, written in language that appeals to MBAs, and framed from a 30,000-foot, corporate-headquarters perspective. There's nothing wrong with the newsletter, really, as long as it's only distributed to the 15 people in the executive suite for whom it's written.

But the company prints 50,000 copies of the publication and sends it to all employees, who glance at it politely, wondering what any of the content—about the company's strategy for Asian business development, progress a task force has made on leveraging currency fluctuations, and a 1,500-word Q&A with the vice president of supply—has to do with them.

The newsletter, which, by the way, is expensive and time-consuming to produce, is what one of Alison's clients calls "vanity press."

Not our role model: Narcissus

Remember the ancient Greek myth about the beautiful young man named Narcissus? The guy was good-looking, all right: kind of like a cross between a young Robert Redford, Brad Pitt, and Heath Ledger. One day, Narcissus went to a pool to get a drink of water and happened to catch a glimpse of his own reflection. He stopped short, mesmerized. He had simply never seen anything so beautiful as his image. He was so smitten, in fact, that he literally couldn't eat or drink or even move. Naturally, this didn't work out in the end, but boy, was Narcissus happy staring at himself for as long as it lasted. He had finally found his soul mate, after all.

From the story, we now have that useful adjective "narcissistic," which means "excessive love or admiration of oneself," according to the *American Heritage Dictionary*. When you're creating communication, ask yourself, "Are we in danger of staring too long at our reflection? Does this communication really serve the audience's needs? Or is it too focused on extolling our virtues?"

"It happens all the time," says this client (who would prefer to remain anonymous because she relies on her paycheck to feed her family). "Some senior vice president has a 'brilliant' idea for an e-mail announcement or a newsletter article, starring him—or occasionally, one of his colleagues. Naturally, we have to comply, because we work for him. And once the communication occurs, people in the executive suite love it. It validates their existence. But it means almost nothing to the person down in the organization, trying to do his job every day."

The problem, of course, is that communication like this is not focused on the needs of the audience—it's all about the guy who is commissioning it.

"Who we are"

Even sophisticated companies and the advertising agencies that support them sometimes fall into the "all about me" trap. For example, recently we were waiting in an airport and our attention was caught by a beautiful billboard, which showed a gorgeous photograph of a modern office building. Okay, so far—they got our attention—but then we read the copy:

> **Who is helping more than 35,000 of the nation's buildings stay safe, comfortable, and energy-efficient?**
> **We are.**
> **We're Siemens, a global innovative company that helps the needs of businesses and communities right here in the United States.**

We are sure that Siemens, one of the world's largest electrical engineering and electronics companies, is a very fine firm. And we suppose we could have dropped everything to figure out what this ad had to do with us. But the ad was all about them—"we're this; we're that"—and not about us.

So instead of spending time trying to figure out what we were supposed to do with the information, we went to buy a magazine—one that had "you" (meaning us) and "how to" on the cover.

▶ **WHAT TO DO INSTEAD** Know your audience, and make your communication all about them. See Chapter 2 for how to do so.

Sin 2: Trying to cover too much

Ever listen to one of those interview shows on National Public Radio where the host alternately interviews guests and takes calls from listeners?

Next time you do, notice how people who are experienced at being interviewed—politicians, celebrities, book authors, activists—tend to be very good at answering questions by delivering a single, focused message. (They may be so good at getting their message across, in fact, that they don't actually answer the question asked, but turn the question to suit their needs.) In any case, by the end of the interview, these experienced communicators have gotten their point across, whether that point is "vote for me" or "buy my book" or "pay attention to this issue."

By contrast, it's likely that at least some of the average people calling in to ask a question or make a comment are

23 different messages

Steve Peha, a partner the Word Factory, a company that teaches writing, tells this story about his challenges in promoting his own firm: "I give my clients advice about having a single, focused message, so I know that's the right thing to do. But when it came to promoting my firm, I felt that there were so many things I wanted to say. I had so much to offer. There was so much I could do for clients."

As a result, Steve found himself creating promotional content that was all over the map. "I finally asked a colleague to help me narrow it down to 1 or 2 main messages. Because, of course, I know that prospective clients can't absorb 23 different things about what you do—they need to know the 1 or possibly 2 things you're all about."

ramblers. They start on one topic, meander over to another, and finish somewhere else entirely. Some seem to be so thrilled to be on the radio, that they can't seem to get over their excitement enough to find a focus. One sentence morphs into another, in a kind of free-flowing fugue. And, in the end, you wonder what they meant, anyway.

▶ **THE POINT**   Unless you have a single focus, you're in danger of not getting your message across at all.

▶ **WHAT TO DO INSTEAD**   Decide on a single high concept for your communication, and focus on getting that message across. See Chapter 4 for how to do so.

Sin 3: Using complicated, abstract concepts

As we've said several times before in this book, too much education is a dangerous thing, especially when it comes to communicating clearly. We feel like we have to use all those words we memorized for the SAT, ACT, or other achievement tests. We try to seem more impressive by constructing complex sentences, with lots of punctuation. We think the more obtuse we sound, the more people will pay attention.

The result is a paragraph like this, which has been adapted from a real opinion piece in a real business publication (but modified to protect the well-meaning person who created it):

> *A common concern within organizations exercising cost control is that project teams are under-resourced. Even armed with the most thorough*

⚠ WORDS THAT MEAN ALMOST NOTHING

Either they're so overused or they're so abstract that they've lost their meaning. You know the ones. Words such as:

Communication

Quality

Paradigm

Synergy

Strategic

So avoid them whenever you can—and, if you absolutely must use them, provide a definition.

strategy, messages may get lost in the general noise of the business. It's intriguing that some businesses continue to support costly scattershot communication channels instead of opting for smarter, customer-driven messaging. By adopting strategic practices, encouraging ownership, and introducing self-governance, communication practitioners can improve penetration through empowerment.

Eeek! Flashbacks of Frankenstein's monster, constructed from mismatched body parts and the wrong darn brain. (Now the monster is running through the countryside, terrorizing farm animals and small children.) The person who wrote the opinion piece was trying to make a persuasive argument about something . . . we're just not sure what. But instead of using tangible examples to make his or her case, the writer loaded up the article with abstract, ethereal concepts. As a result, we have no idea what they are talking about.

▶ **WHAT TO DO INSTEAD** Make your communication tangible and specific. See Chapter 5 for how to do so.

Sin 4: Losing the human element

Why is so much communication created as if there were no human beings involved—despite the fact that we are attracted to stories about people? We don't know the answer, either, which is why we can't explain the following e-mail announcement that was sent to all employees at a *Fortune* 500 corporation. (The following has been modified from the original, including being cut by 50 percent to eliminate some of the pain.)

INTRODUCING OUR NEW STRATEGIC DIRECTION

Over the past few months, we have been working diligently to address three sets of issues: strengthening our management team, fixing our operational and financial problems, and forging a new strategic direction to begin repositioning Acme for the future. We previously have communicated our significant progress on the first two issues, and this e-mail reports on the excellent progress we have made on the third initiative: setting a strategic direction for the new Acme.

Assessing Our Strategic Position

As you know, the Strategic Coordination Team, led by Chief Investment Officer John Doe, has spent the past four months researching and analyzing different strategic options for Acme. Assisted by Ace Management Consulting, the team reviewed in detail the work of the strategy teams assembled in 2000 and developed new and insightful product profitability analyses. The team also conducted rigorous financial and competitive analyses; and met with dozens of experienced sales, operating, and staff managers at both corporate and regional locations. This enquiry helped develop our new strategic direction.

Strategic Direction

Our new strategy will center on providing distinctive, consumer-oriented products and services to members in targeted markets. This more customer-segmented strategy is not intended to be a radical departure from the past, but will have important implications about how we will manage our business.

By focusing more sharply on the customer segments that align with our strengths and offer the best profit potential, we will be

(continued)

better able to provide consumers with a wider range of product choices, including more open access products. We will make it easier to understand and access our services by making them simpler and more efficient.

Next Steps

Now that we have defined a preliminary strategic direction, we must begin the hard work of making that strategy a reality. Multiple issues must be addressed, ranging from clearer definition of account and member needs by market segment, to better product linkage, to aligning resources to support the new direction, to defining a specific timetable. Careful planning and crisp implementation of the new strategic direction will be paramount.

The senior management team and I are excited and encouraged by our definition of a preliminary strategic direction. However, corporate strategy is much more than declaring what direction the company should take. To turn strategic plans into marketplace success, actionable priorities must be clear; and the company's resources focused to support, refine, and implement the strategy.

Please be assured that as we move forward on the strategic direction, as well as the operational transformations under way, we will keep you informed about our progress. I urge you to take the time to fully understand the changes Acme is making and formulate your own plan to help us meet them. If we are to succeed, each of us—each department, each individual—must fully understand and support our goals. Success will come from doing the right things, in the right way, every day. Thank you again for your continued support.

Nobody talks like this

You'd think that quoting real people would be a great opportunity to bring people's stories into communication, breathing life and interest into what you're trying to convey. It's a shame, then, that so many quotes we see read like this: "Thanks to the outstanding vision of John Smith, the company remains well-positioned in the industry with a balanced portfolio of advanced products and services for a wide range of applications." Nobody really talks like this. It's just corporate speak. We'd like to hear the real guy's real voice—then we'd pay attention.

What a great opportunity this would have been to tell a story about the company's efforts to turn itself around. Instead, we get this corporate drivel, which is neither engaging nor inspiring. Communication like this is simply a sin.

▶ **WHAT TO DO INSTEAD** Tell stories that are real and human. See Chapter 6 for how to do so.

Sin 5: Creating a dense thicket of information

Those of us communicating in the twenty-first century are pretty darn lucky. We've got tons of tools right at our fingertips: word processing, presentation and graphics software, the ability to post information on Web sites, and lots of other ways to make our content well-organized and visually appealing.

That's why there's no excuse for the following example, adapted from a major corporation's actual communication, but shortened to protect you, our beloved reader, from terminal boredom.

NEW OPERATING STRUCTURE OF MANUFACTURING ANNOUNCED

The new operating structure and its benefits

To achieve our corporate vision of being the most admired company, we need to be the best at delivering high-quality products that meet our customers' needs. Recognizing that this requires the collaboration and expertise of many areas, we are creating a new Manufacturing organization, to be led by Chuck Paisley.

The Manufacturing operating structure is more than a reorganization; it is the framework for a collaborative relationship among Supply, Quality, and other supporting functions to achieve common goals.

Key elements of the operating structure include:

- Operating Units focus on product families or regions by bringing plant managers and dedicated functional leaders together. These units enable alignment of priorities, the facilitation of decision-making, and the ability to leverage our resources to achieve the objectives of that product or regional group.

- Functional Units enable the sharing of best practices across Operating Units, establish common standards, and develop functional excellence in our processes and people.

- Plants report directly into an Operating Unit and are part of the decision-making process for determining objectives and how to achieve them. Plants execute using their own leadership team, including site functional expertise, and draw support from the functions within their Operating Unit.

Transitions, Timing, and Next Steps

Many positions within the Operating and Functional Units are still being defined. The Global Leadership Team is developing job descriptions with the intent to fill positions as rapidly as possible.

Many one-on-one conversations will be occurring as we progress through this phase. The process is to look internally first for people who have the technical skill set and who also are adept at motivating others, building and managing peer relationships, building effective teams, and managing with vision and purpose. They will be action-oriented to drive results, customer-focused, and able to delegate effectively, while embracing our values and exhibiting managerial courage.

If you have any questions about the process, the skill set being sought, or the positions themselves, you can forward your questions to Stan Dixon, who will ensure that they are directed to the appropriate person for response.

If you're like us, your reaction is, "Huh?" It's really, really dense—and we only gave you about half of what was there originally. If ever a communication begged for a map, an organizational chart, or other visual aids, it's this one. And although bullets are used, there are still way too many meandering sentences and thick paragraphs. In a word: laborious.

▶ **WHAT TO DO INSTEAD** Make communication easy to navigate and use visuals to convey your concepts. See Chapters 7 and 8 for how to do so.

Sin 6: Going on too long

Tell them what you are going to say.
Say it.
And tell them what you said.

That is probably the best advice we have ever heard about making a speech. It is effective when it comes to speaking, because your audience has little frame of reference when you get up to talk. They don't know what you are going to say, or even how you are going to say it. (Are you going tell jokes? Scream? Express outrage? Will there be PowerPoint, a video, nothing?)

By telling them up front what you are going to say, you set the stage for the message that follows. And reviewing what you said at the end allows you to hammer home your message, since the audience will have nothing to refer to or study once you are done speaking.

All this explains why the "tell them what you are going to say . . ." method is so effective.

Perhaps too effective. Given the success in the speech arena, people in other communication arenas

By telling them up front what you are going to say, you set the stage for the message that follows. ▶▶

are sometimes tempted to use the same formula. But that is *not* an effective approach.

What works in speeches doesn't work in other forms of communication because:

A. It's not necessary in print publications or online because the audience can go back and review earlier points with ease (if they want to).

B. The audience doesn't have time or patience for it.

▶ **WHAT TO DO INSTEAD** Say what you need to say as briefly and simply as possible. See Chapter 9 for how to do so.

Sin 7: Lecturing and hectoring

We want you to succeed in all your communication efforts.

And we've tried to think of everything we could possibly share to help you do so. If we've sometimes resorted to nagging, we apologize, and say: Don't do as we do, do as we say. Lecturing and its even more annoying twin, hectoring, are not effective ways to grab an audience's attention, because people hate to be talked to as if they're 8th graders and you're the vice principal.

Here's an example of what we mean: The following isn't from a CEO, executive vice president, senior vice president, or even a department head. It is from a high school principal. But it is a perfect example of how *not* to communicate.

It has all the delicious attributes of really bad "official" communication: authoritative tone, "corporate speak" (or its academic equivalent), and a rules-based, off-putting style.

We have included the entire letter. Our commentary is in brackets.

Dear Parents of Students attending the Senior Prom:

It has come to the high school administration's attention that some of our students who are planning to attend the senior prom on Friday, April 8th, are also planning not to attend school on Monday, April 11th.

It is my responsibility to inform you that Monday is a regular school day. Students not in attendance will be counted as truant.

For the second time this year I have heard students and parents discussing the nonexistent tradition of senior cut day. Please note that there has not been a senior cut day since my arrival at the high school four years ago.

[This is classic leader hubris—if he says something, it must be true—despite the fact that everyone else has a different reality. In fact, the school does have a long-standing tradition of senior cut days. But the principal is trying to stop the tradition.]

Personally I take the mandate of the Board of Education seriously to protect all of our students. Discussions with my fellow high school administrators and our faculty council has brought forward the conclusion that students who choose to violate the attendance policy on Monday should lose senior privileges and should not be included in upcoming senior activities. They are also subject to high school attendance consequences and removal from participation from sports programs on Monday and Tuesday. I would hope students' parents would strongly consider making the appropriate decisions concerning school attendance.

[We apologize for including the whole painful paragraph but if we took anything out, you wouldn't get the full flavor of the communication style: We're Going To Hit You Over The Head Repeatedly Until You Get The Point. Bam! Bam! Bam! Ready to cry uncle yet?]

(continued)

On Friday, April 8th, at 11:30 I will be meeting with all prom participants to review the areas I have discussed above. Further, I will be speaking about another potentially dangerous and harmful tradition: "the keg race." I truly believe that if we allow this tradition to continue we are just a short time away from a potential tragedy.

[Notice he doesn't tell us what "the keg race" is. We guess he assumes that we know? We didn't, so naturally we went to our favorite 17-year-old and asked. It turns out the "keg race" is another senior tradition ("No, it's not," the principal would say) in which seniors attempt to drink more beer in a finite period than the class that came before them. Last year's class drank the equivalent of 104 kegs of beer between January 1 and graduation, so this year's goal is 105 kegs—or more.

As issues go, this one seems more problematic than cutting school for a day. And maybe this is, in fact, the real issue/reason for the principal's letter, but you can't tell from how this is structured.]

With all of this in mind, I invite senior parents and parents attending the senior prom to attend our meeting on April 8th (along with all prom participants) to review the areas I have discussed above. We will be meeting in the auditorium at 11:30. I believe your attendance will go far to influence our children to follow school policy and be safe.

[Maybe we're bad parents (or people), but this letter doesn't make us feel responsible—it makes us feel incredibly irritated. The admonishing tone makes us inclined to think the issues at hand may be blown a little bit out of proportion; thus, we're tempted to dismiss the whole thing altogether. Still, we had a good laugh with our favorite 17-year-old. It was a bonding experience. I guess we should thank the principal for bringing the family closer.]

Don't you feel lectured to? Don't do this.

▶ **WHAT TO DO INSTEAD** Provide instructions, not a lecture. See Chapter 10 for how to do so.

➡ INSIGHT 11:
The best 4 years of your life

You can pray for us.

As you read, we have 3 kids in college. One of them is at a state school—thank you, Lord—but the other two go to places where *one* semester costs more than a nice mid-sized car.

The fact that we have 3 in college simultaneously explains 2 things. Why we: don't take vacations or eat out very often and why we are so familiar with college recruiting materials.

And we say this with grudging—given what we pay per semester, it couldn't be anything other grudging— admiration: College recruiting material is among some of the finest communication we have ever seen.

Really.

And what works for them can work for you.

If you emulate the 4 things that they do extremely well, we can't guarantee that you too will gain an endowment of hundreds of millions of dollars, but we can promise that your communication will become much more effective.

Consider what they do:

1. *All the materials are appealing.* The layout, typefaces, and use of pictures make you want to see what they have to say. You can't communicate anything unless

you get someone's attention, and just about every bit of college recruiting material—even for schools we know our kids have no interest in attending—has gotten our attention.

2. *College recruiting material is focused.* Colleges know they are appealing to 2 different audiences: kids and their parents (the ones writing the big checks). There isn't a word, picture, or image that doesn't address either (or both) of those audiences. (And when talking to one specific group, like parents, the material is self-contained, so that the kids can skip over it.)

3. *Questions are anticipated.* What is the male-female ratio, average class size, approach to teaching? What can I major in? Are there going to be people like me? How does financial aid work? All the typical questions a student (or his parent) might have are addressed right up front.

4. *There is a call to action.* The material always tells you how to learn more (who to contact; the address of the Web site), how you can get a specific question answered, and how you can apply.

This is very effective communication indeed. We have the (tuition) bills to prove it.

12 | Sell the new approach

Now that you've read this book (and seen the light), you're ready to put these attention-grabbing approaches into practice. But first you may have to convince your boss, client, or other stakeholder that change is good—that communicating differently will be effective. In this chapter, we'll provide you with strategies for doing so.

THE VICE PRESIDENT of communication was driving her staff crazy. Maybe Maureen's problem was that she graduated from journalism school several decades ago. Or that she never missed a word of the *New York Times*. Or that her favorite movie of all time was the 1976 film *All the President's Men*, about how *Washington Post* reporters Woodward and Bernstein investigated the details of the Watergate scandal, leading to President Nixon's resignation.

In any case, Maureen was a devotee of old-school journalism, and such a stickler for a "gold standard" of communication that she seemed to her staff to be inextricably stuck in the past. The tone of all communication had to be factual and objective. Sentences had to be grammatically flawless, and paragraphs perfectly constructed and complete. There would be no shortcuts: Maureen frowned upon breakheads and sidebars as pandering to the audience, and even looked askance at charts and graphs, since they weren't "real writing." To Maureen, communication was a higher calling that shouldn't be sullied by tricks or gimmicks.

For people in her department who were under 35, or who specialized in electronic communication, Maureen was maddening. She was smart, no doubt, but she didn't seem to grasp that the world had changed, and communication had changed with it.

Luckily for her staff, Maureen eventually retired (I think she's at her farm in Vermont, trying her hand at small, well-crafted novels), but you may face a similar obstacle—someone who still believes in a 1950s-idea of "the right way"—in your quest to make your communication audience-focused.

Here's how

Don't worry; we can help you overcome the obstacles to achieving good communication. In fact, we're going to offer you 4 strategies for making your case and, as a bonus, one important thing *not* to do. Here goes.

Start small

As Bruce Springsteen wrote, "From small things, mama, big things one day come." When it comes to communicating differently, we think you should heed his advice.

Here's what we mean: A lot of what's in this chapter relates to the official communication you need to create: the brochure, the organizational e-mail, the big client meeting. But you actually spend most of your time communicating informally: for instance, sending an e-mail to a colleague.

So to demonstrate how to communicate differently, do it every day. Make your personal communication an example of the principles we've demonstrated in this book, including: **Know your audience and meet their needs. Choose a single focus and stay on message. Be brief.**

You won't be hitting people over the head with "a new way of doing things" but you'll be quietly demonstrating how well the new way works.

Bruce would approve.

1. Buy extra copies of this book and give them to people (page 207).
2. Use best-practice examples to persuade (page 208).
3. Provide evidence to make your case (page 210).
4. Make a persuasive pitch (page 212).

And the "don't":
Don't go on and on as if you just invented communication (page 214).

1. Buy extra copies of this book and give them to people

We may be accused of shameless self-promotion, but we figure what's good enough for Oprah—who promotes her magazine on her show and vice versa—and Heloise (as in "Hints from . . ."; see Chapter 10)—who gives suggestions on how to buy her book—is good enough for us.

We advocate that you buy and distribute extra copies of our book not only because it helps us (actually, it mostly helps our publisher, but we like our publisher), but also because of what we've discovered in our own consulting work: Books by experts do have an influence, especially to people over 30.

Books have built-in credibility—unfortunately, they're more credible than you are. You could say something a hundred times and no one pays attention, but if the same advice is in a book, suddenly it's taken seriously.

So quote us. Excerpt us. Paraphrase us. Invite us to speak at your organization. (See our Web site *www.your attentionpleasebook.com* for how to arrange that.) Use us. We like it.

 **OTHER BOOKS TO QUOTE**

We've quoted authors and experts throughout this book and provided a list of resources at the end (see page 219). Here's a short list of books we think you'll find especially helpful:

Gonzo Marketing
by Christopher Locke

Information Anxiety
by Richard Saul Wurman

Why We Buy
by Paco Underhill

The Design of Everyday Things
by Donald A. Norman

Influence: The Psychology of Persuasion
by Robert B. Cialdini

2. Use best-practice examples to persuade

- Which publications does your boss read and rely on?
- Where does your client go on the Internet to make purchases? Obtain news? Look up information?
- Which consumer magazines does the senior vice president receive at home?
- Are there companies the CEO admires for their marketing and branding efforts?

Knowing the answers to these questions can be the foundation for convincing people that it's time to communicate in new ways. Here's why: Effective media and marketers are using many of the attention-grabbing techniques we've described in this book. By showing your stakeholders how communication they admire employs these techniques, you can prove how persuasive and compelling the new ways can be. For example:

- The *New York Times*, not known as an innovator, is using color to liven up its pages.
- The *Wall Street Journal*, hardly a trendsetter, is breaking up long columns of copy with breakheads, sidebars, and visuals.
- Business marketers are using storytelling and other humanizing elements to sell equipment and software.

Best of best practices

Does your senior management admire anything that General Electric does? Does IBM's marketing campaign make your vice president's heart beat faster? Does someone in your department wish the company could be a little more like Apple and a little less like the Kremlin?

Benchmarking against the best—and then creatively borrowing their approaches—is an old trick, but it's also one that works. So feel free to cite best practices as a way to sell your proposed communication approach.

Here are some guidelines:

- **One size does not fit all.** Although it's helpful to know how world-class companies like FedEx and HP communicate, you can't expect to use their solutions as is. You need to adapt best-practice concepts to fit your culture, geography, and industry.

- **Today's best practice is tomorrow's old hat.** As external factors (such as technology, employee needs, business expectations) change, best practices also evolve. Never stop searching for new innovations and solutions.

- **Look first within your own organization.** Especially if you work in a large organization, there are likely to be folks somewhere in your world who are trying to tackle the same kinds of problems that keep you up at night. These ideas may not be the most innovative, but their major advantage is that they are proven to work in your organization.

- **Widen your search.** When exploring best practices, don't miss an opportunity to look beyond the usual suspects (large, well-known, "Most Admired" companies) to study more unusual organizations. For example, the U.S. Army has some terrific best practices in leadership communication. And fast-growth companies are often taking unconventional approaches.

3. Provide evidence to make your case

There's a simple way that will help you make your case: Use *evidence*, which we define as factual information that helps in forming a conclusion.

Many of us associate evidence with "research"—we think it takes considerable time and significant budget to gather the facts. But it doesn't have to. There are many different ways to get the information you're looking for: from formal research to leveraging data from other sources. Try these methods for collecting evidence:

- **Existing research.** Reports and white papers published by consulting firms and research organizations are the easiest and least expensive way to get your hands on findings. Take advantage of what's offered free online (if it's from a reputable source), or pay a modest amount for this information. Also, newspapers and business periodicals frequently have articles summarizing research on different communication trends. For example, if a large percentage of your audience members are in their 20s, you can access research on this group's technology preferences to bolster your argument about why, for instance, it's so important to communicate using new media such as cell phones and podcasting.

- **Observation.** Watching how people experience communication is a simple way of getting to know your audience better. For example, for decades retailers have been using "mystery shoppers" where an observer assumes the role of customer to collect information on

Sports Illustrated for . . . young adults?

Many years ago, Time Inc. was thinking about creating a new version of *Sports Illustrated* aimed at young people aged 8 to 15 based on *Sports Illustrated*.

The folks working on the project were confident about the concept, but they were struggling with what to call the new publication. *Sports Illustrated for Teens*? *Sports Illustrated for Young People*? *Sports Illustrated for Boys and Girls*? *Sports Illustrated for Children*?

Early on, of course, someone suggested *Sports Illustrated for Kids*, but the people in the room—most of whom were in their 40s or 50s—rejected it out of hand, maintaining that the name was patronizing toward the demographic.

One of the team members went home after the meeting and told his 11-year-old daughter—a sports nut if there ever was one—about the meeting and asked her what she thought.

"'Dad," his daughter asked, "why don't you just call the magazine *Sports Illustrated for Kids*?"

"But, sweetie, don't you think it is insulting to be called a kid?"

"Dad, I know I am a kid."

Armed with that great piece of evidence, the next day the team member called the researchers, who went out and conducted focus groups that confirmed that kids did indeed consider themselves kids.

The magazine had a title, Time Inc. had a successful launch, and the power of evidence was proven once again.

the shopping experience as it relates to selection, environment, and customer service. You can employ the same methods to get information about distribution, access, the value of communication displays, consistency of messages, or any other dynamic.

- **Quantitative research.** Many of us associate research with tedious, all-encompassing surveys. But it's possible to conduct a small, manageable survey, using an online tool like Zoomerang or Survey Monkey, by selecting a representative sample of your audience members and asking them targeted questions.

- **Focus groups.** An old favorite, focus groups can explore an issue in depth, allowing for expressive dialogue about the topic being studied. As a result, they yield valuable insight into what people perceive and believe. Although focus groups do not result in statistical data, verbatim responses captured during focus groups are a powerful indication of what audience members think.

4. Make a persuasive pitch

You've bought this book and shared it with others. You've found best-practice examples. You've compiled evidence. But you can't relax yet—now you need to pull it all together to create a persuasive pitch that will convince your stakeholders to support your proposed approach.

We've found that this is often where people get tripped up, because they assume that the facts speak for them-selves. That's why we provide these tips on how to present your recommendation to ensure buy-in.

- **Make sure you have your opinion leaders' attention.** Focus and engage the folks you're trying to persuade by starting out with something that will immediately get their attention: a story, a visual, a quote, or an amazing fact. Relate what you're going to talk about to their needs or concerns.
- **Establish a need.** It's all very well and good that you care about communication; why should they? Introduce

a challenge or issue that needs to be resolved, and discuss the ramifications if the need isn't resolved. Then really hit home by describing how the need impacts your audience on a personal level. Make it vivid and believable by telling a story or providing facts that help make your case.

- **Propose a solution.** Now that you've got them on the edge of their seats by getting their attention and establishing a problem, here's your golden opportunity to provide the solution. Focus on the WIIFMs (What's In It For Me) by describing how each individual will benefit. Draw from past experiences to describe past situations where a similar approach was successful. And although you'd like a free exchange of ideas, you also don't want to get bogged down in objections—so anticipate possible concerns and address them as part of your solution.

- **Paint a picture.** Visualization is one of the best tools you have in your persuasive toolbox. Use it when describing your proposed solution by helping your audience visualize what life will be like when your plan is implemented. Help them picture how things will change for the better, and remind them of the consequences if things don't change.

◀◀ Visualization is one of the best tools you have in your persuasive toolbox.

- **Call for action.** As they say in Hollywood, time for the boffo finish. Summarize your message by reviewing steps 1 through 4. Don't assume because people are not disagreeing that they've agreed, so ask for their support. Demonstrate your own commitment by outlining the steps you are taking to implement the plan. And, finally, issue a call to action by telling the audience what they need to do to make the vision a reality.

What not to do: When enthusiasm is a bad thing

Paul is not normally an outgoing guy. In fact, his stepson, Sam, does an absolutely spot-on impression.

"This is Paul when he is happy," Sam says with a perfectly neutral expression on his face.

"And here is Paul when he is sad," continues Sam without changing his expression.

We tell this story because of what happened to Paul recently and how it is instructive about how you should *not* try to sell this new form of communication to your bosses and peers.

After complaining for months that his vision seemed to be getting worse, Paul went to the ophthalmologist who discovered that Paul had cataracts in both eyes.

Now, cataract surgery these days is no big deal, and the operations went off without a hitch.

But an interesting thing happened after the successful surgery: Paul could suddenly see without the glasses he had worn since 8th grade—a fact that he shared with those around him.

Once.

And again.

And again. And again. And. . .

Finally, after a week of listening to Paul point out that he could see the time on the alarm clock without his glasses and he could watch television from across the room, his family threatened to drag him back to the surgeon and demand an operation that would restore his poor vision.

Paul, finally, got the message. He has not mentioned his improved vision in at least an hour.

We tell this story because one of the natural inclinations of discovering something new and wonderful that benefits your life is you want to share it with the world. The problem is the rest of the world has its own concerns and doesn't want to spend more than a nanosecond or two hearing about why *your* life is better.

What they are searching for is information that will help *them*.

That's why in trying to get across the benefits of this new way of communicating you need to stress what is in it for your audience. (It's all about them. Sound familiar? It should. If it doesn't, revisit Chapter 2.)

➡ INSIGHT 12:
"You can observe a lot by looking"

You may not agree that Baseball Hall of Fame catcher Yogi Berra is the font of all knowledge, but for Alison, his words helped provide the spark of inspiration that would grow into this book.

It all started in a tornado-proof conference room at a manufacturing plant outside of Dallas.

Alison was in the middle of conducting a focus group with employees of a large corporation to find out about their communication preferences, when the tornado warning sirens sounded. Luckily, it was just a drill—something this East Coast gal had never before experienced—but everything stopped while other employees entered the room to comply with the safety exercise.

Naturally, this interruption broke the thread of the discussion. So when the drill was over, Alison decided to improvise a little activity to help the 12 participants refocus.

She handed out the latest issue of the company employee newsletter, which people in the group hadn't seen.

"Here's what I'd like you to do," Alison explained. "For the next couple of minutes, look at the newsletter the same way you'd usually do—and then I'll ask you a couple of questions about what you think."

As the employees complied, Alison watched them. And she was surprised to see that:

- No one in the group looked at the front page first. Most went straight to the back page, where there was a roundup of company news organized by division and location.
- Once participants started flipping through the issue, they never went back to reading the newsletter in a linear way from front to back. They skipped around, pausing when they found an item that interested them.

Alison realized that employees looked at the newsletter the way they wanted to experience it—not the way the communicator designed it.

That meant that many of the company's assumptions about the publication weren't true. For instance, employees didn't consider the lead article (first story on page 1) the most important content. And they didn't treat the newsletter as a valuable resource, but as a casual FYI. And they had no intention of reading every word—skimming to get the gist of it worked just fine.

And then it was as if the image of Yogi Berra appeared, right there in Texas. First he said, "It ain't over until it's over."

And then he said, "I really didn't say everything I said." And then he said, "You can observe a lot by looking."

That's when Alison realized that she, and anyone else whose job depends on communication, needed to spend a lot more time observing what the audience actually does with what we send them. Does the business customer immediately open the envelope that holds the brochure or let it sit in his inbox for days? Does the e-mail recipient print the long message instead of looking at it onscreen? Does the teenager look at the Web site while watching television while playing a video game while sending a text message on her cell phone?

And, once you see what's actually happening, Alison realized, the next step is to think about what to do differently in response to these real-world behaviors. This book is the beginning. Now you need to listen to Yogi, and get out there and see what's going on with your audience.

Once you do, you'll understand how to grab their attention.

Resources

But Wait! There's More! by Timothy Samuelson
▶ Inspiration from the master of the infomercial, Ron Popeil

Don't Think of an Elephant! by George Lakoff
▶ How to shape political messages—or any message—to be more compelling

Follow The Yellow Brick Road by Richard Saul Wurman
▶ Instructions deconstructed

Gonzo Marketing by Christopher Locke
▶ Thinking outside the box to market a product, service, or idea

Influence: The Psychology of Persuasion by Robert B. Cialdini
▶ The definitive book on using psychology to persuade

Information Anxiety by Richard Saul Wurman
▶ Diagnosis of and treatment for information overload

Love is the Killer App by Tim Sanders
▶ Leveraging love to persuade and influence

The Market Research Toolbox by Edward F. McQuarrie
▶ Marketing research 101; great for beginners

The Mother Tongue by Bill Bryson
▶ Using words more effectively by building on the origins of English

Selling the Invisible by Harry Beckwith
▶ If you can sell an intangible, you can sell anything; Beckwith shows you how

Why We Buy by Paco Underhill
▶ A book that seems to be about shopping, but is really about effective selling

Writing Copy for Dummies by Jonathan Kranz
▶ Simple guide to smart copywriting

YOUR ATTENTION, PLEASE.

Index